NEEDLES & NOTIONS

Paper-Pieced Patterns *with a* Sewing Room Theme

Jaynette Huff

Martingale & Company
Bothell, Washington

Credits
President . . . . . . Nancy J. Martin
CEO/Publisher . . . . . . Daniel J. Martin
Associate Publisher . . . . . . Jane Hamada
Editorial Director . . . . . . Mary V. Green
Design and Production Manager . . . . . . Cheryl Stevenson
Technical Editor . . . . . . Laurie Baker
Copy Editor . . . . . . Karen Koll
Proofreader . . . . . . Liz McGehee
Illustrator . . . . . . Laurel Strand
Photographer . . . . . . Brent Kane
Text Designer . . . . . . Trina Stahl
Cover Designer . . . . . . Magrit Baurecht

MARTINGALE & COMPANY
PO BOX 118
BOTHELL, WA 98041-0118 USA
WWW.PATCHWORK.COM

PRINTED IN HONG KONG
04 03 02 01 00 99 6 5 4 3 2 1

Martingale & Company

That Patchwork Place

That Patchwork Place is an imprint of Martingale & Company.

Mission Statement

We are dedicated to providing quality products and service by working together to inspire creativity and to enrich the lives we touch.

Dedication

This book is dedicated to my husband, Larry. I am thankful every day for his continual love, support, encouragement, and presence in my life. And also to my sister, Martha Beth Palmer, whom I love, and who has always been there for me. (I know there is a quilter within her trying to get out!)

Acknowledgments and Special Recognition

Irma Gail Hatcher, the friend who continually encourages me with her warmth and understanding, her astute suggestions, and her quick enthusiasm.

Patty Galas, who paper foundation pieced so many of the blocks for the samples. I would never have finished on time without her. What a joy to have a fellow paper foundation piecer so close at hand.

Valerie Schraml, my computer hero. She led the way through the manuscript. Thank you! Don't put away your fonts or disks—we may need them again.

To the women who work at Idle-Hour Quilts and Design, an especially warm thank-you for giving me the time off from the shop to sew and write . . . sew and write . . . sew and write.

And to all those quilters who participated in the original "Sewing Room Block-of-the-Month" program. I greatly appreciated your enthusiasm. You are why this book exists!

Library of Congress Cataloging-in-Publication Data

Huff, Jaynette.
Needles and notions : paper-pieced patterns with a sewing room theme / Jaynette Huff.
p. cm.
Includes bibliographical references.
ISBN 1-56477-289-6
1. Patchwork—Patterns. 2. Miniature quilts. 3. Sewing in art. I. Title.
TT835 .H794 2000
746.46'041—dc21 99-053397

CONTENTS

PREFACE

SEWING AND QUILTING are, for me, an ever-evolving journey down a creative path filled with tools and equipment, colors and textures, fabrics and friends. Paper foundation piecing is the part of that journey that I am currently enjoying. This book is a recognition and sharing of that part of the walk with fellow sewers and quilters, all of whom are on their own special sewing journeys. It is my hope that you find my "journal notes" helpful and fun as you walk along your own creative path.

My first introduction to sewing fabric onto a paper foundation was in a class taught by Eileen B. Sullivan (The Designer's Workshop, Duluth, Ga.) at a local guild in 1994. My piecing direction was changed forever! This technique lit a fire under me! I felt an immediate bond to and appreciation for the process and its results. I shall always be grateful to Eileen.

As an owner of a quilt shop in Conway, Ark. (Idle-Hour Quilts and Design), I had the wonderful opportunity to further hone my paper-foundation-piecing skills and share the technique with many other people. Early on, these paper-foundation-piecing classes filled over and over again. It was like the light dawning as people saw the magic, the ease, and the usefulness of this new approach to piecing. The problem was not in the method or how to do it; it was in when to quit!

Not only did I love the method and enjoy sewing on the few patterns available at the time, but I began to convert every pattern I could to paper foundation piecing. If I could count it, I could sew it. Again, fellow enthusiasts followed suit. Soon the shop began offering a class in numbering: converting basic patterns and blocks to the foundation format. (The class was, and still is, called "Numbering 101.") There are a lot of quilters who want to take more control of their quilting lives and projects, and making their blocks and patterns work for them as they want is one step in that direction.

Then the ultimate urge emerged: I wanted to design and execute my own paper-foundation-pieced patterns. I wanted to see my own designs sewn on fabric, using this technique. Fortunately, many people have responded to my designs through class sign-ups. Early patterns included basic fictional characters and figures, such as a Christmas nutcracker, an angel, and "Sewing Room Sue" (see page 52). They have also focused on buildings and houses within small landscapes, such as a winter cottage, a gingerbread house, and a whole Victorian village. A fairly recent pattern direction has been toward constructing full-sized quilts of paper-foundation-pieced landscapes (70" x 70" and larger). I enjoy the challenge of designing more intricate paper-foundation-pieced blocks and patterns, linking landscapes and architecture.

Several other fictional character types were formalized into a book in 1996 *(Holiday Heroes)*, co-authored with a colleague of mine, Carol Stearle. All of these were fairly large-size patterns of characters such as Uncle Sam, Johnny Appleseed, and Santa. The book also featured smaller 4" companion blocks (i.e., a star for Uncle Sam, an apple blossom for Johnny Appleseed, a Christmas wreath for Santa).

Today, many quilters seem to be interested in stitching smaller quilts and wall hangings; 4" companion blocks are just the right size for such projects. In addition, as more and more people understand the basics of paper foundation piecing, their ability and desire to piece more complicated blocks have increased. A small block with several different parts does not seem quite so intimidating anymore.

At Idle-Hour Quilts and Design, we do several block-of-the-month programs, but most are template oriented or strip pieced and rotary cut. With the interest in paper foundation piecing swirling about me, this was a natural. I wanted to offer a paper-foundation-pieced block-of-the-month program, and I wanted to design the blocks myself. But what twelve blocks? What size? What theme? Lots of questions went through my mind, but the important question was, "What are my customers interested in?" The answer? Sewing and quilting. There it was!

The twelve Needles and Notions blocks featured in this book are the result of that block-of-the-month program. Originally they were presented as 4" blocks to be pieced five times each and arranged in a row-by-row setting. The quilt "Sewing Room Sampler: Row by Row, Notion by Notion" (page 63) is the end result of that block program.

Once the program ended, however, Idle-Hour was still receiving requests for the patterns. What to do? How to make the blocks and patterns available to more people? Put them into a book.

Thank you to Martingale & Company for viewing my blocks and part of one quilt, seeing the potential in these designs, and then encouraging me to write them all down, create new arrangements and settings, and share them with you.

It is with great enthusiasm and excitement that I present them here. I most sincerely hope you find them a fun and welcome addition to your own sewing room, and that the whole paper-foundation-piecing process moves you forward on your own sewing and quilting journey.

Step out! Join in! Get moving!

INTRODUCTION

Needles and notions,
Fabrics and time,
Blended together—
Sewing so fine!

WELCOME TO MY sewing room! Your arrival here represents a journey that all quilters make as we experience the joy of learning and sharing various sewing techniques. The process used here, paper foundation piecing, is not the end of the journey, but rather a pleasant stop along the way. It is a wonderful place to explore and experience, a place to breathe deeply, to take it all in and to make it part of what we do as sewers and quilters.

Defined, paper foundation piecing is "an organized step-by-step process of piecing fabrics together in alphabetic and numeric order directly onto a foundation on which the sewing lines have been drawn." Sounds a bit tricky, but it really is not.

Not entirely new, the foundation-piecing process has been around in various forms for many years, one of the earlier forms being English paper piecing. Recently, however, the process has enjoyed a sweeping surge of interest and exploration. Sewers and quilters have taken to it again, but have modified and fine-tuned the process, adding new methods and techniques, once more claiming it as their own.

This book is a reflection of that journey and that reclamation as it introduces new (smaller and more detailed) block patterns but still focuses on what is very comfortable and secure to us. It is a walk and an exploration closer to home: our own sewing rooms and the tools of today's sewers and quilters.

Any job we do, any skill we develop, and any activity in which we are interested generally involves using materials and tools designed for that specific purpose—the tools of the trade. Such tools often serve to make jobs and activities easier to manage, faster to complete, and more accurate and precise. The tools of sewing and quilting are no different. Ever since we first began sewing and quilting, we have developed and used specific materials and tools. Many have been around for years and years, and we plan never to give them up. And every year we see the introduction of new and improved sewing tools, fabric, and notions. They serve as useful equipment, hopefully leading to greater quilting creativity and sewing success. And we want to try them all!

But for most sewers and quilters there are a number of basic notions and tools that are "must haves." We simply cannot do without them. For example, picture the sewer without her needles and pins, threads and scissors. Visualize her without her iron and ironing board, seam ripper or tape measure. Or take away the ultimate tool of all, her sewing machine! Deprive her of these tools (and perhaps several others), and imagine the results. She would sorely feel the loss!

Between the covers of this book are the patterns for twelve paper-foundation-pieced blocks representing sewing tools and notions: a button jar, iron, needle, pincushion, rotary cutter, scissors, seam ripper, sewing machine, spools of thread, tape measure, thimble, and a cup and saucer for a cheery cup of tea. Each can be used alone or in a variety of combinations to create small wall hangings and quilts.

Because I appreciate paper foundation piecing, it was important to me that these blocks be paper foundation pieced. But as paper foundation piecing has now become a fairly well-known process, it was further important that these blocks be a "stretch" for sewers into the world of the smaller, the more detailed, and the more precise. Thus, there are two different block sizes provided: 4" and 6". First-timers, begin with the 6" blocks, but do not be put off by the smaller blocks. They are well worth the effort.

In addition to the notions blocks, you will find Sewing Room Sue—Dreaming and Quilting, a block representing a dream version of how we might spend our time in our sewing area: sitting and quilting. (Too bad it is only a vision for many of us at this time.) "Sue" is a salute to an old favorite quilt block design, Sunbonnet Sue, but she is new and improved here as she rocks and quilts to the beat of paper foundation piecing.

All of the blocks have been presented in a variety of quilt arrangements and settings, from the very simple one-block quilt to the more complete combinations of "Sue" amidst all her "needles and notions." May they be a pleasant stop on your sewing walk.

GETTING STARTED

Tools and Supplies

THERE IS AN almost overwhelming selection of sewing supplies and equipment available for today's quilter. Below, you will find a listing of items that are useful to paper foundation piecing as it is presented in this book.

- All-purpose thread for machine piecing blocks and borders. Choose only good-quality, 100% cotton thread. A neutral tan or gray works well with most fabrics.
- Batting
- Beading needle for attaching bead embellishments
- Beads for embellishing several Needles and Notions blocks (commercially available)
- Colored markers for making reference marks on your foundation paper. Fine-line markers in four to

five different colors are recommended.

- Darning foot or open-toe appliqué foot for free-motion machine quilting
- Design wall. This tool is optional but you will find it very helpful when deciding overall block placement.
- Embroidery floss for block embellishment and outlining details (commercially available)
- Even-feed or walking foot for straight-line machine quilting
- Fabric markers to draw the extended seam lines on the wrong side of the fabric for the 1/8" borders. Depending on the fabric color, you may need one for dark fabrics and one for light fabrics.
- Freezer paper, the recommended paper for the foundation pattern (commercially available)
- Iron and ironing board. Set up an ironing area within easy reach, as you will use it following every fabric addition. An iron with a steam setting is preferred.
- Light box. This handy tool makes it easier to trace the pattern onto freezer paper, as well as to transfer embellishment placement lines onto the pieced unit. You may also use a window, or create your own.
- Machine quilting thread. YLI or Sew-Art nylon monofilament is recommended. Use clear for light fabrics and smoke for dark fabrics.
- Mechanical pencil for tracing the pattern onto freezer-paper foundation
- Pins. Extra-long, glass-head silk pins are recommended. Use them to secure the parts together when matching pieces and later for sashing and border attachment.
- QuilTak tacking gun and tacks for quick basting and machine quilting
- Quilting needle, hand or machine (quilter's preference)
- Rotary cutter, cutting mat, and rulers. Select a mat no smaller than 17" x 23" and a small- or medium-size cutter. A 6" x 24" ruler with 1/8" marks is necessary for cutting strips; for trimming pattern parts, you will need a 6" x 6" ruler. If desired, purchase a 12½" x 12½" ruler for squaring-up your work.
- Safety pins for possible pin-basting. Use size 0 or 1 only.
- Scissors, one good-quality pair that you are willing to use for cutting both paper and fabric. Smaller 5" embroidery size works especially well for easy pick-up and trimming. Thread clippers are also helpful.
- Seam ripper (optional, but probably necessary)
- Sewing machine in good working condition. A simple straight-stitch machine with reverse capability is all that you need. The recommended stitch length is fifteen to twenty stitches per inch.
- Sewing machine needles. A size 80/12 or 90/14 is recommended for paper foundation piecing.
- Stiletto. A sharp, pointed instrument that helps separate stubbornly adhered paper and fabric pieces.
- Trash bag for trimmings
- Tweezers for removing the paper foundation in tiny, hard-to-reach corners and crevices

Fabric Selection and Preparation

ONE OF THE most enjoyable activities in the whole quilting process can be choosing fabrics for your project. It is a time to "graze around" in the quilt shop and fabric store, waiting in anticipation for that special fabric to reach out and grab you, saying, "Choose me! Use me!" It is a time of letting that initially chosen "theme fabric" lead the way toward other fabric selections. Your choices will build on one another.

Yet many quilters find selecting fabrics the hardest part. They have a very tentative and cautious attitude when it comes to choosing what to use. Will this fabric work? Do these fabrics go together? How many should be used? For this reason, this section offers some guidelines and suggestions for fabric selection and preparation. These guidelines have frequently proven to be quite helpful, and if you are a bit apprehensive when it comes to fabric selection, consider trying them.

- Use only top-quality, 100% cotton fabrics. Cottons truly make your work easier because they tend to behave with each other. Quilting takes too much time to waste on poor-quality fabrics that will disappoint you later.

- Provide contrast in value, scale, and intensity (see "Basic Color Principles" below).
- Look for the following types of prints, as they tend to work well with smaller blocks.

  Tone-on-tone prints. Although there is a subtle design and texture to the fabric, from a distance they tend to read as solids. They do not cause confusion or design misunderstanding.

  Tiny allover prints. These include such designs as pindots, mini-florals, and mini-geometrics. They add visual interest and texture, yet due to their small size, they do not distract or confuse the viewer.

  Coordinated companion blenders. These are the companion fabrics within a larger fabric collection that are often called blenders. They coordinate with and complement each other, and take away some of the worry about "do they go together?" Yes, they do.

  Solids. These fabrics have no texture or design; thus they cause no distortion or confusion. They may be lacking in interest, however.
- Approach the following prints with caution. There is nothing inherently wrong with these prints, but if you use them, work with them carefully. Perhaps the suggestion ought to be, "Don't not use them, just use them intelligently."

  Directional prints. In paper foundation piecing, directional prints can be difficult to control and place and can lead to confusion. The smaller the block is, the more confusion that can result.

  Large-scale prints and geometrics. These may overpower the small pieces, causing viewer distraction.

  Big plaids and bold stripes. Again, the large scale may be inappropriate for such small blocks.
- Let outside influences in. Consider choosing and using your fabrics based on selection criteria other than the fabrics themselves. Here are some suggestions:

  It's a mood and an attitude. Make spontaneous, go-with-the-flow fabric selections. Choose a few fabrics to get started, then add colors and prints as the need arises. Let the blocks speak to you about appropriate color and number. Be bold and inventive. Be responsive and adventurous.

  Be scrap-happy and reminiscent. Let your blocks reflect past quilting endeavors, and clean out your scrap bag! What fun to see the scissors block made from fabrics from your latest baby quilt. Remember that pincushion fabric? It was left over from your daughter's graduation quilt. And so on.

  Create variations on a theme. Choose a theme for your quilt first, then follow through with your fabric choices. Choose fabrics that repeat and reinforce that theme, creating greater emphasis and impact. Possible themes might include patriotism, holidays, or historical periods.

Basic Color Principles

Value. Value is the difference between the lightness and darkness of fabric colors. Within your quilt, you need to incorporate fabrics of light, medium, and dark values. Of course, value is a relative term. The fabric of darkest value in one quilt may be of only medium value in another.

Scale. Variety in fabric scale adds interest to a quilt. Scale refers to the size of the designs printed on the fabrics. When choosing your fabrics, select large-, medium-, and small-size prints. Of course, scale, like value, is relative. What is considered small in one quilt may be medium in another. Further, what is appropriate scale will vary with factors such as block design and piecing technique. Due to the small block size in these patterns, large-scale prints are probably inappropriate for the blocks, but not for the borders.

Intensity. How brilliant or intense are the colors of the fabrics chosen? A little bit of bright or strong intensity can go a long way, but its absence can bury your quilt in dullness and boredom. It can be a touch of color intensity that makes your quilt eye-catching and memorable.

Let one color dominate. Choose one particular color to serve as the predominant determinant (i.e., blue), and then select additional fabrics that are shades and gradations of that same color ranging from light to dark. Such a range of one color causes your quilt to glow and shimmer.

Border it. What goes around, comes around! Let the last fabric to be used in the quilt be the first one chosen. Border prints can do all the work of color selection for you. The fabric designer has already created both the color palette and the various proportions of colors within that palette. You already know it works because you were drawn to it in the first place. Border prints go one step further: They pull it all together later when they are actually used as the outer border. The border fabric can determine factors such as border width (i.e., the amount of the border print you wish to include in the border becomes the width). The unused part of the border print can also serve as sashing and/or corner posts.

The ultimate fabric selection guide: Use colors and fabrics that please you. Trust yourself! Enjoy your particular combination.

- Buy enough. It is often hard to determine exactly how much of each fabric you will need for these projects. Sometimes you can simply look at the block and know that a tiny 6" x 6" scrap is all you need. However, when you are trying to purchase enough for all your background areas, it becomes more difficult to pinpoint exactly the amount needed. The yardage will vary depending on experience and amount of trimming away. Better to purchase extra than not have enough.
- Prewash your fabrics. Avoid the heartache of shrinkage and dye runs that might occur later.

Learning Foundation Piecing Terminology

WHEN LEARNING ANYTHING new, it is always wise to learn the language and be able to "talk the walk." Brief explanations of the terminology to be used help the learning process by providing a common ground of understanding.

This section contains brief definitions of the various terms and phrases encountered in this walk through paper foundation piecing. Several definitions contain specific page references to more complete, detailed explanations.

ACCENT BORDER. A reference to the use of the ⅛"-wide border presented in "Accenting the Positive" (page 17).

BINDING. The recommended binding strips are cut on the straight grain and double folded. When applied to the quilt, they finish to ¼" wide with mitered corners. Refer to "Finishing Touches" (page 20) for a more complete discussion.

CONTRAST. Refers to something that exhibits differences when compared with another (i.e., contrast in color, contrast in scale, contrast in value, etc.).

DASHED LINES. Used to separate the pattern parts (page 13).

FABRIC KEY. The table provided with each pattern that lists all fabrics needed and their accompanying alphabetic symbol. Each fabric symbol is encircled to differentiate it from the Sewing Order symbols. Example: (BK) means background.

FOUNDATION PATTERN. That pattern on which you actually sew. It contains the sewing lines and parts, as well as the fabric symbols. It can be a variety of forms, but the recommended type in this book is commercially available freezer paper.

HASH MARKS OR REFERENCE MARKS. Pre-sewing marks that are added to your foundation pattern on every dashed line. The rule is, "Dashes need hashes." Later, these reference marks will be used to pinpoint match your parts together exactly (page 13).

INTENSITY. A fabric color's degree of brilliance and strength or the degree of color saturation. A touch of intense color goes a long way, but a "popper" fabric can be a good addition.

MITERED-CORNER BORDERS. Attaching your border pieces in each corner of the quilt such that the seam line creates a 45° angle. Refer to "Making Borders with Mitered Corners" (page 20).

PAPER FOUNDATION PIECING. An organized step-by-step process of piecing fabrics together in alphabetic and numeric order directly onto a foundation on which the sewing lines have been drawn. Refer to "Step by Step to Successful Paper Foundation Piecing" (page 11).

Part. An organized collection of pattern pieces, separated from each other on the pattern by short dashed lines.

Piece. The smallest unit within a pattern. Makes use of only one fabric piece.

Pin-Checking. A quick test to see if enough fabric has been allowed for flipping up later with complete coverage of a particular pattern piece. Involves pinning along the proposed sewing line and then checking, by flipping up the new fabric piece, to see if the additional fabric will be big enough (page 14).

Pinpoint Matching. A technique for ensuring that the pattern parts are correctly aligned. Using the hash marks, poke a sewing pin straight through the top of a hash mark and into the fabric of one part, then into the corresponding hash mark of the part you are attaching. If correctly aligned, they will match (page 16).

Reverse or Mirror Image. This is the orientation of the foundation pattern. It is the wrong side of the finished project. The design on the foundation appears as a reverse image of the final project.

Scale. The size of the designs printed on the fabrics. Use a variety of small, medium, and large scales in the fabrics of your quilt.

Sewing Order. The step-by-step listing of the order in which you sew or piece the pattern. It is the alphabetic and numeric road map to the piecing of each pattern (i.e., Part A: 1–4).

Squaring Up. The process of ensuring straight sides and 90° angles in the corners.

Staystitching. Stabilizing the outer edges of your pattern block with a line of stitching 1/8" from the edge. Keeps the bias edges of your block or wall hanging from stretching until you can add borders or binding.

Straight Lines. Used to indicate separate pattern pieces within parts. Straight lines indicate sewing lines. Do not cut along these lines.

Straight-Set Borders. Attaching your border pieces in a consistent stair-step, or log-cabin, format (see page 18).

Swatch Chart. A visual guide to your Fabric Key. Actual pieces of fabric are attached to the chart and identified with the corresponding alphabetic symbol.

Value. The difference in degree between the lightness and darkness of colors. Use a variety of light, medium, and dark fabrics in your quilt.

READING THE DIRECTIONS

ALONG ANY PATHWAY or route, it is always a good idea to take the time to find out where you are headed. The process of sewing and quilting is no different as we encounter different methods and new techniques for creating our works of art.

This section contains three sets of directions: "Step by Step to Successful Paper Foundation Piecing"—a very specific guide to the paper-foundation-piecing process; "Accenting the Positive"—directions for incorporating the 1/8"-wide accent border into your quilt top; and "Finishing Touches"—steps for moving your quilt top to the final stages of embellishment, basting, and quilting.

Stop a moment and read through each section, concentrating on gaining the overall picture. Later, as the need arises, refer to the directions as you actually encounter the need for specific hints and suggestions.

Step by Step to Successful Paper Foundation Piecing

Step 1: Make a Swatch Chart

The first step in the paper-foundation-piecing process is an organizational one: Make a fabric swatch chart for easier fabric control and identification. Although you may be tempted to skip this step, don't! It pays for itself later when many different piles of colored fabrics and scraps surround you and you cannot remember which green is the particular one you need. Also, as the patterns become more elaborate and you need more fabrics, it becomes more difficult to keep track of them all. The swatch chart can bring some order to the chaos!

On the following page is a sample swatch chart. Add the identifying labels and letters beneath each box. Tape, glue, pin, or staple a corresponding fabric piece in each box.

The rule to remember is "Check your swatch chart twice; sew only once." This is a good rule to follow with any sewing project.

Step 2: Trace the Pattern onto the Foundation

Trace the desired block pattern onto your paper foundation. You have several choices of material to use for the foundation, including standard typing paper, bleached newsprint, tear-away stabilizer, or freezer paper. Commercially available freezer paper is recommended here due to its superior adhering qualities. After you iron the fabrics to it, they tend to remain tidily tucked out of the way. (The directions assume you will use a freezer-paper foundation, but they also apply if you use another foundation.)

This book includes a foundation pattern for each block design. The foundation pattern has all parts labeled with the sewing order and fabric designations. This is the pattern on which you actually sew. Notice that it is the mirror image of the finished block; everything appears in reverse order. This is as it should be, because you sew on the wrong side, or the paper side. When you turn your work over to the fabric side, you see that everything is correct.

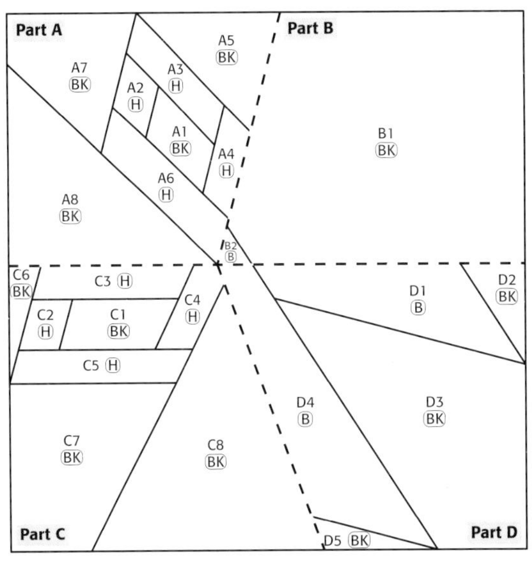

Foundation Pattern

When tracing your foundation pattern, it is helpful to use a light box or tape your pattern to a window. If you have a table with a center leaf, make your own light table by removing the leaf, placing a piece of glass across the opening, and putting a lamp underneath. If you are using freezer paper, remember to trace the pattern on the paper side, not the shiny, plastic-coated side.

After tracing all the lines (both straight and dashed), be sure to re-label and re-number each piece carefully and accurately. Please note that the alphabetic and numeric designations provide you with the Sewing Order (i.e., A1, D5, E4), while the circled letters indicate fabric (i.e., (BK) means to use the fabric designated for the background).

When you have finished tracing, cut out the entire pattern or block. Trim away any excess foundation paper from the outer edges.

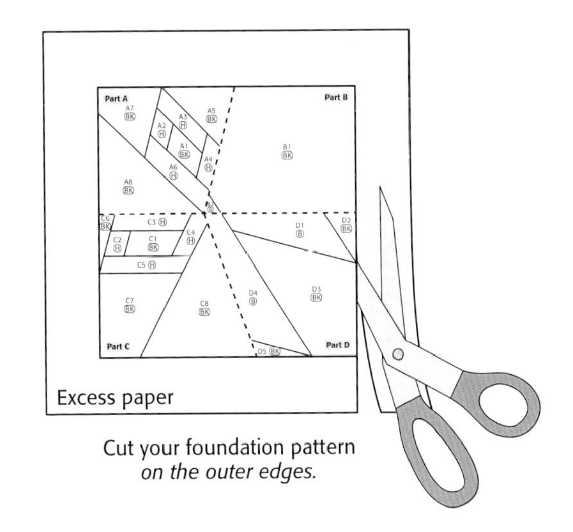

Cut your foundation pattern *on the outer edges.*

*Sample Swatch Chart**

*Note: Make photocopies of this sample swatch chart and use it for each of your projects.

Step 3: Add Reference Marks to Your Foundation

Adding reference marks, or hash marks, to your foundation is another step that should be preceded by the words, "Do it now, because it more than pays for itself later!" Trust me on this.

On each pattern, solid lines or dashes separate individual pieces and parts. Solid lines separate pattern pieces within parts. Do not cut along these lines (with the exception of the outer edge of the pattern itself). These are your sewing lines! Short dashed lines separate parts of the pattern within particular blocks. Later you will be cutting the parts apart along the dashed lines.

Solid lines = Sewing lines

Dashed lines = Cutting lines

Every dashed line should have reference marks added across it. These marks will later serve as the precise matching points between parts when joining them together. Remember the rule: Dashes need hashes. If it is a dashed line, it should receive reference marks. Make use of many different types of reference marks: single slash, double slash, triple slash, single X, double X, etc.

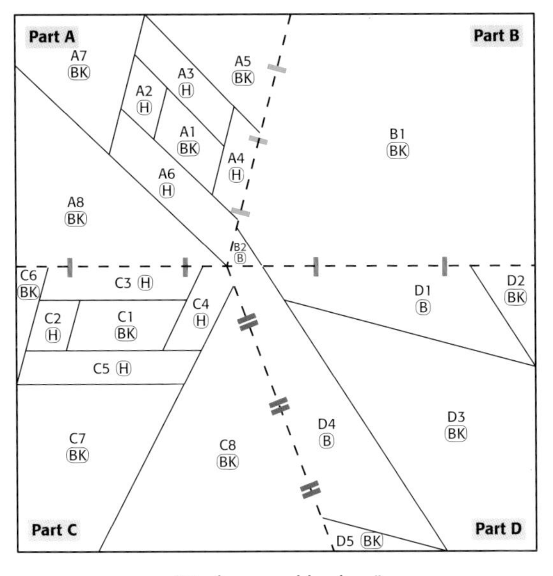

"Dashes need hashes."

Any marking tool is acceptable, but be sure to use several different colors so matching is easier. Avoid yellow, as it is difficult to read. I find that Crayola thin-line washable markers work well.

Step 4: Refer to the Sewing Order

Every pattern comes with a Sewing Order. This is a step-by-step listing of just exactly the order in which to piece or sew the pattern. It tells you what you should sew first and what to do with it when it is finished. It tells you when to join various parts together. It is basically a road map to the piecing of each pattern, giving you the correct piecing and placement order.

As you follow the Sewing Order, place a check mark before each step as you complete it. This becomes a handy reference for knowing where you were when you stopped last. (How many of you have sat down at your sewing machine after being away from a project for several days and been unable to remember where you left off? This check-off system will get you right back on track.)

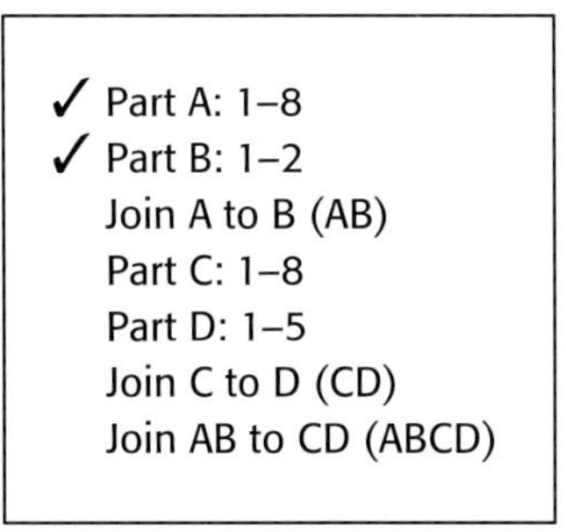
✓ Part A: 1–8
✓ Part B: 1–2
Join A to B (AB)
Part C: 1–8
Part D: 1–5
Join C to D (CD)
Join AB to CD (ABCD)

Sample sewing order for Scissors block with check marks

Step 5: Cut Out the First Part

After consulting the Sewing Order, locate the first part listed. Remember, in paper foundation piecing you work both alphabetically and numerically. The larger the pattern, the more parts there will be. Your Sewing Order will tell you what is first. Whatever it is, find the first part on your foundation, and with your scissors, carefully cut it out. Attempt to cut exactly on the line. Remember, cut only on dashed lines, not on straight lines. Set the rest of the foundation sheet aside.

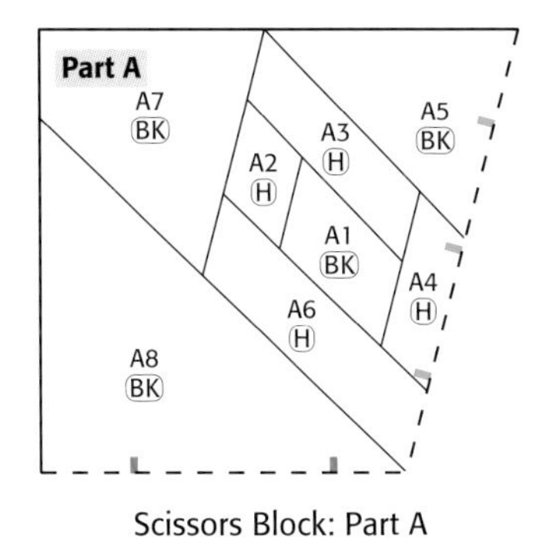

Scissors Block: Part A

Step 6: Iron the First Piece

Locate the first piece, A1, and its corresponding fabric (check your swatch chart!). From your fabric, roughly cut out a piece large enough to cover that area completely with at least a ¼" seam allowance all around. When in doubt, err on the side of too large. With the wrong side of the fabric to the shiny side of the freezer paper, iron the first piece in place.

Note: *This is the only piece that is ironed in place before it is sewn.*

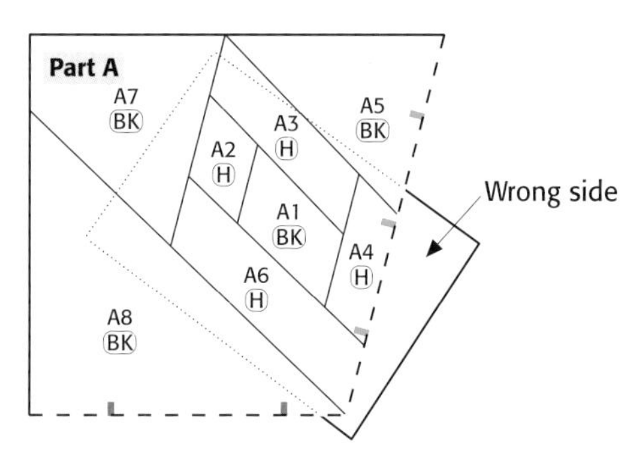

Step 7: Begin Sewing

Look at your foundation to determine which fabric is indicated for the second piece. After consulting your swatch chart, cut a piece of fabric large enough to cover the piece. Do not try to cut fabrics the exact size of the piece. Instead, use large-enough pieces to ensure coverage, with extra for seam allowance. You will be trimming away the excess and frequently can use the leftovers in another place.

In this process, do not concern yourself with grain line. If such concern is important, indicate the direction on your foundation with an arrow and carefully adjust the fabric placement so the grain line is aligned with that arrow.

Hold the foundation so the paper side is facing you and the attached fabric piece #1 is behind it. Rotate the paper so that A1 is below A2. Locate your sewing line. It is the solid line running between piece #1 and piece #2. Right sides together, place piece #2 over piece #1 with at least ¼" of fabric extending beyond the sewing line. With the foundation paper side facing you, hold the whole unit up to the light to see if you must reposition your fabric. At this point, most of piece #2 will be behind piece #1.

Note: *The previously sewn work will always be below the line you will be sewing on.*

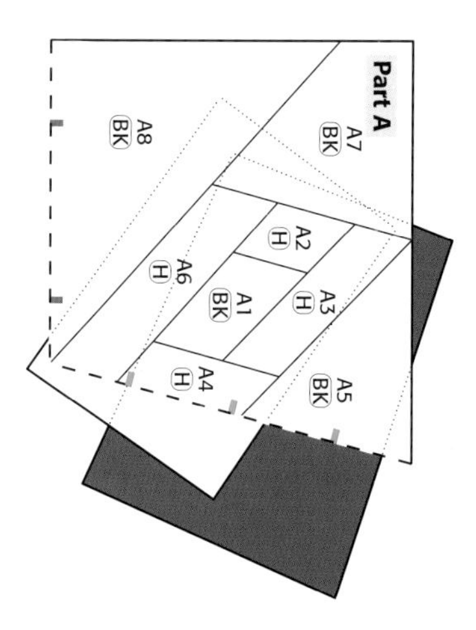

Again, make sure that the fabric piece you are adding will be large enough to cover the area it is designed to cover, plus extra for seam allowance. Too big is better than too small. It is better to waste a bit of fabric than to have to remove stitches and start again. If you are unsure that your new piece is large enough, test it first. Simply pin the new fabric along the proposed sewing line and flip the fabric up. You can now truly see whether it is the correct size. This takes only a few seconds but is well worth the effort. (Pin-checking takes a lot less time than ripping out fifteen to twenty stitches per inch!)

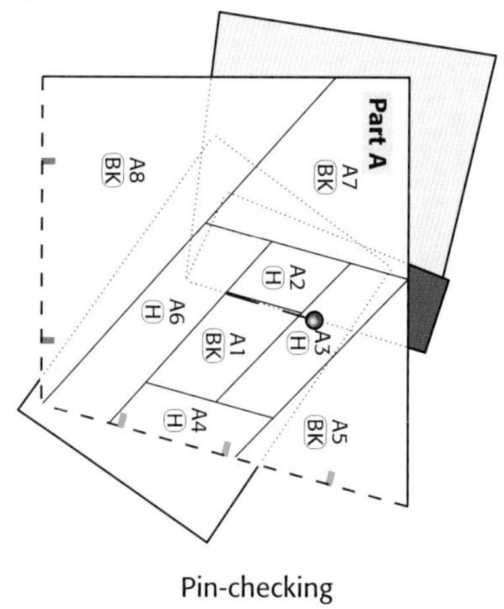

Pin-checking

With the foundation paper side up, sew along the length of the seam over the pattern line, using fifteen to twenty stitches per inch; backstitch, if desired. The purpose of such small stitches is to make the removal of the paper foundation easier.

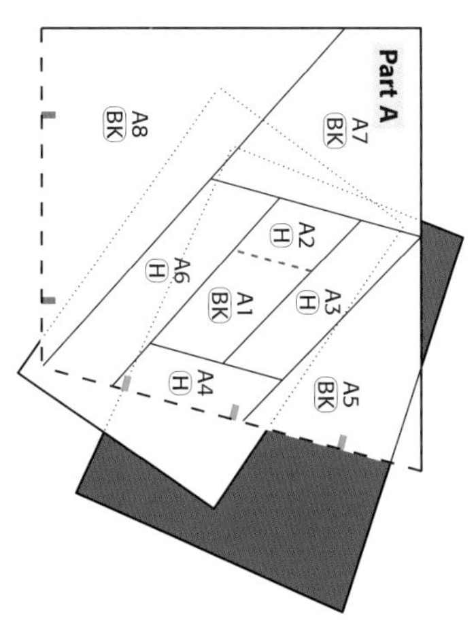

Step 8: Trim the Seam Allowance

Remove the unit from the machine and lay it flat on the table with the foundation side up. With your fingers holding down the previously sewn fabrics, which are still right sides together, carefully fold back the foundation at the sewing line. Using your thumbnail, crease the foundation paper along the sewing line. Do not flip up the fabrics yet! Pick up the unit and trim the fabric layers to a scant ¼" seam allowance. Use a small pair of scissors and simply eyeball the ¼" trim, or use a rotary cutter and ruler, if desired.

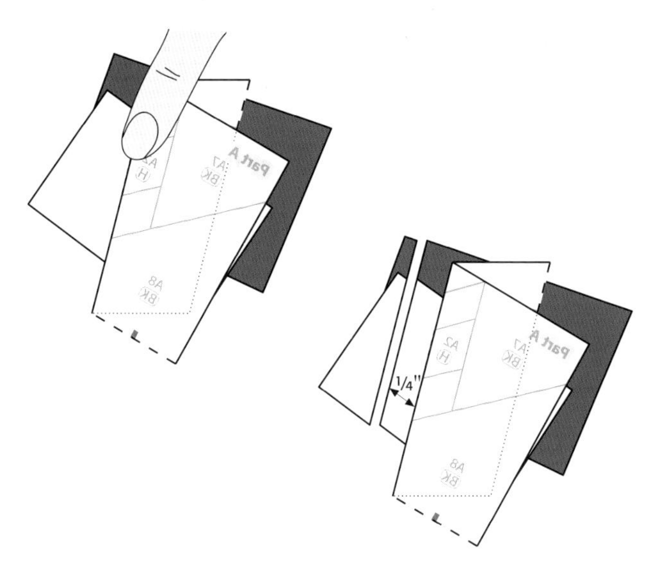

Step 9: Flip and Press

Once you have trimmed the fabric, fold the foundation paper back down. Flip up the newly attached fabric piece and iron it into place, ensuring a sharp, creased fold along the seam line. Press from the paper side first, gently pulling on the new fabric piece as you glide the iron toward your hand and over the paper. Then flip the whole unit over and press from the fabric side. This allows you to check for excess fabric folds or pleats on the seam line.

Check to make sure the entire pattern piece is covered with plenty of extra fabric around the sewing lines. This excess is your seam allowance. If you have lots of excess fabric, carefully trim it away, but make sure you leave plenty around the edges of the piece. Keep the trimmed pieces for possible use later for smaller pattern pieces.

This is where the advantage of freezer paper's adhering quality is very apparent. The freezer paper holds the fabrics exactly where you have pressed them and keeps them out of your way.

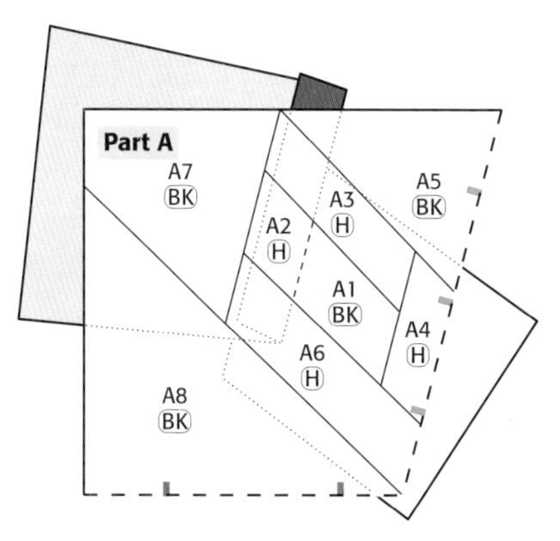

Step 10: Repeat the Process

Continue in this manner until the entire part is completed. With each new fabric piece, refer to step 7. Remember to sew the pieces in numeric order or they won't fit together correctly. Continue with step 11 once the entire part has been sewn.

Step 11: Trim the Finished Part

Once a part has been finished, trim an exact ¼" seam allowance around all of the sides. As accuracy counts here, use your rotary cutter, mat, and ruler. Do not eyeball this seam allowance.

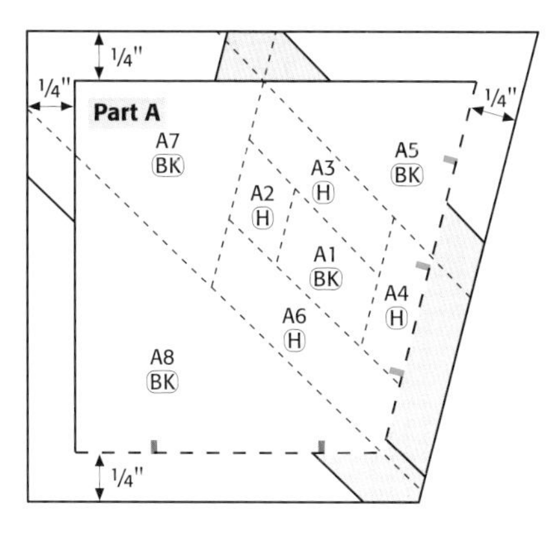

Next, check the Sewing Order. You may be instructed to set this part aside, to go on to the next part, or to join parts together. It all depends on where you are on the pattern.

Step 12: Join the Parts

Once several parts are complete, it is necessary to join them together accurately and precisely. This is where those reference marks from step 3 really pay off.

First, carefully align the appropriate parts with their corresponding reference marks (i.e., single red slashes align with single red slashes; double blues with double blues, etc.). Hold them with the fabric right sides together.

Next, pinpoint match the reference mark. Insert a pin through the hash mark on one part, then through the fabrics and into the paper of the other part. Ideally, the pin will line up exactly and pierce the corresponding mark on the other piece. If it does not, simply reposition the pin until it does. Remember, these are bias edges, so they will ease right in. Add as many pins along an edge as needed for exact placement.

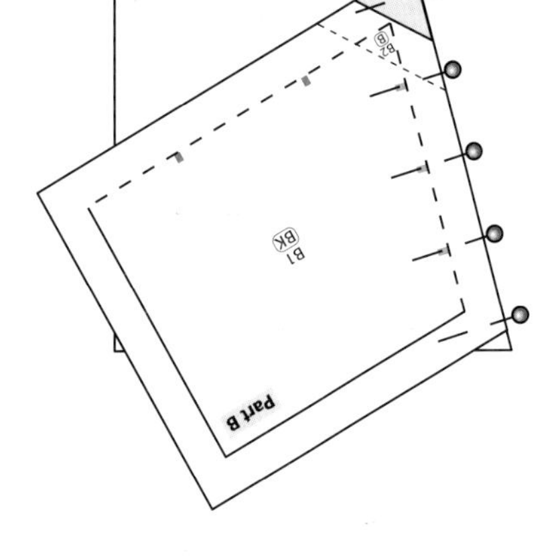

Sew along the pinned edge. The needle should just barely brush the paper's edge. Sew carefully, slowly, and accurately. Do not remove the pins until the last moment; otherwise, you will lose your perfect match as the pieces shift or slide away from each other.

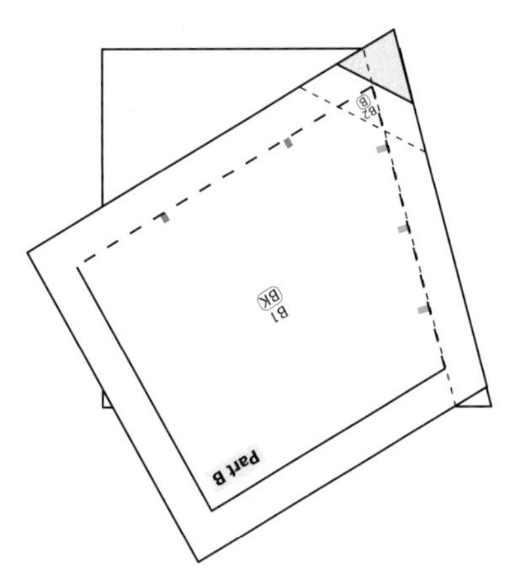

Remove the unit from the sewing machine and check to make sure the points match precisely.

Step 13: Press the Seam Allowances

Once the parts are sewn together, press the seam allowances. The general rule is to let them go where they want to go. Press toward the direction of least resistance. If needed, press the seam allowances open to spread out the bulk of several parts coming together at the same point. Continue in this manner until all parts are completely joined together, checking the Sewing Order for guidance.

Step 14: Remove the Paper

Do not remove the foundation paper from the outside edges of a part until it has been joined to other parts or until the outer edges have been joined to sashing or borders. Remember, these fabrics have been cut and placed with no real concern for grain line, so the edges are primarily bias edges and can easily stretch or become distorted. To control this, staystitch ⅛" from the finished block or pattern edges.

Once the part is stabilized by other parts or outer borders, gently remove the foundation paper. Usually the smaller stitch length allows for easy removal, but with tightly adhered pieces, use a stiletto. Gently insert the stiletto point between the paper and fabric and carefully ease it between them, going back and forth to loosen the paper. It may also help to gently bend or roll the paper and fabric unit, loosening the bond between them. Avoid tugging or tearing too hard on the seam lines and stitches.

Be sure to remove all pieces of the foundation, using tweezers to remove paper from tiny corners or crevices.

Step 15: Add Sashing and Borders

The first border or sashing is the most important one because it stabilizes your paper-foundation-pieced project and corrals all those tiny bits and pieces.

The beauty of paper foundation piecing should be readily apparent in this step because your blocks and designs are truly accurate. If sewn correctly, your points will be almost perfect, and there will be ¼" seam allowances all around. The side measurements should all match, so adding sashing and simple borders becomes a breeze!

For more information on adding borders, refer to "Accenting the Positive" (below).

Accenting the Positive

HAVE YOU EVER admired a framed portrait or picture that had several layers of colored matting? Did those multiple layers effectively frame the picture and force you to focus on the subject matter within? Did you notice the angled cut on the matting and think how the staggered look of the multiple mats actually made the picture better? Or that a particular mat color served as an accent to draw out those same colors within the picture itself?

This same effect can be achieved in your quilts and wall hangings by adding narrow ⅛" borders. One-eighth inch borders you say? Not me! Not now! Not ever!

Wait! The process is really quite easy. It is primarily a process of establishing your sewing line from an inside seam line rather than from the outside fabric edges. Read on . . .

The technique developed for achieving this look was originally inspired from Cheryl Greider Bradkin's book, *Basic Seminole Patchwork.* Although introduced as a method to edge various bands of Seminole piecing strips, it serves as a great technique for framing blocks and small wall hangings, creating precise, even ⅛" borders.

This technique can be used to generate accurate ¼" borders as well. The trick is to measure from an inside seam line, and make sure the new line of stitching is an equal distance from the first all the way around.

All twelve of the Needles and Notions blocks, as well as Sewing Room Sue—Dreaming and Quilting are shown with the ⅛" accent border. In addition, several of the larger wall hangings make use of them (refer to "Tutti-Frutti" on page 66 and "Country Sampler" on page 71).

Step 1: Squaring Up

The process begins by first squaring up your project, whether it is a pieced block, a fussy-cut picture from a pre-printed fabric, or even a small wall hanging ready to have borders added.

Using your rotary cutter and a ruler with right angles (a 12½" x 12½" ruler works well), square-up the work, making sure you have straight sides and accurate 90° angles in each corner.

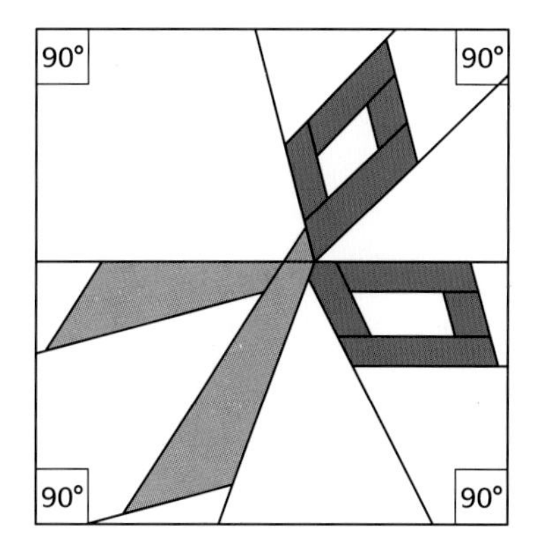

Step 2: Cut the Accent Border Strips

Next, cut ¾"-wide strips from the fabric to be used as your accent border. Although the borders will only be ⅛" wide when complete, cut the strip ¾" wide. (According to traditional quilting techniques, if you want a ⅛"-wide finished strip, add ¼" on both sides, creating a ⅝"-wide strip. However, it is easier to cut and handle a ¾"-wide strip than a ⅝"-wide strip. Of course, this means the outer seam allowance will be ⅜" wide, but this causes no harm. If it bothers you, simply trim the seam-allowance width after you sew it.)

Step 3: Cut Other Border Strips

Cut the border following the accent border the width desired plus ⅝". For instance, if you wish the next border to finish to 2", cut your strips 2⅝" rather than the more traditional width of 2½". Set these aside.

Step 4: Create the Accent Border

Accent borders are created using the straight-set technique, so first you must decide the order you are going to use when attaching the border strips (i.e., side-side-top-bottom, or top-bottom-side-side). Neither is better nor more correct than the other, but once you choose an order, remain consistent for all the remaining borders you add. For our purposes here, we have added the sides first, then the top and bottom.

Pressing toward the center will tend to bury the ⅛" border. If you press the seam allowances away from the project, the accent border will stand up over the project, much like actual framing mats do in a picture. The choice is yours.

1. Using a ¼" seam allowance, stitch a ¾"-wide accent strip to each side of the center unit.

2. Press the stitches flat to set them, then press the seam allowances toward the center of the project.

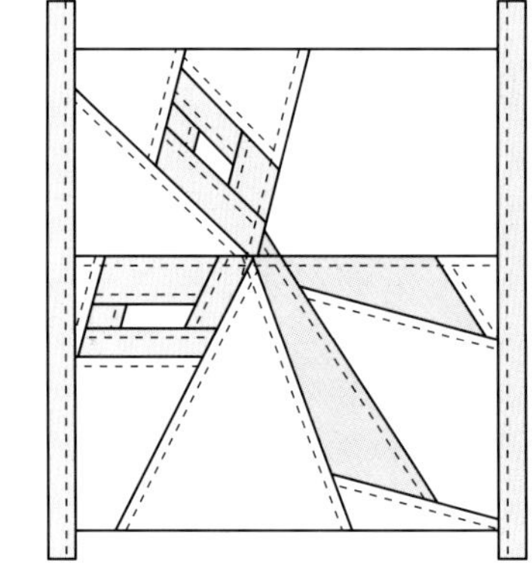

3. Trim the strip ends even with the center block to square up the project again.

4. Add the remaining 2 accent strips to the project top and bottom. Press and trim in the same manner as the side borders.

5. Working on the project wrong side, draw lines to extend the side-strip seam lines to the strip edges. These lines will become the sewing guidelines rather than the outer edges.

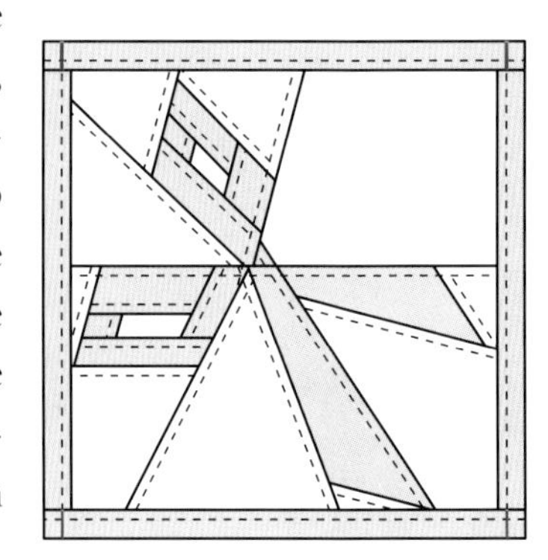

6. Locate the ⅛" guide on your presser foot as shown. You may also use an actual ⅛" presser foot or simply measure and mark the width on your presser foot. Some machines also allow you to move your needle position.

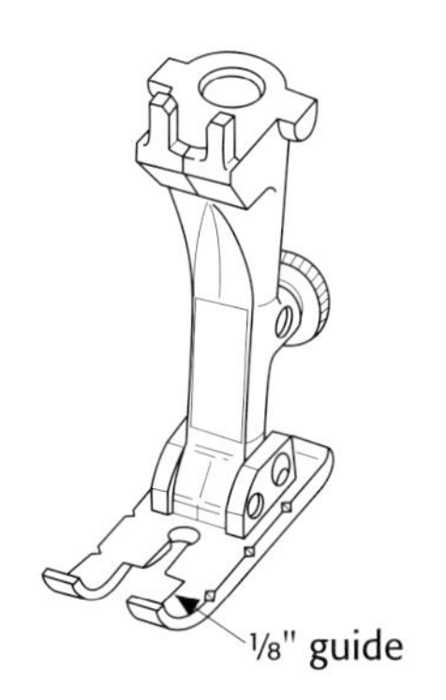

7. Pick up a strip of your next border. Remember, you are adding the borders side-side-top-bottom, so your first addition will be a side strip. With right sides together and edges aligned, place the new border strip under the center unit so the marked guidelines you have drawn in show. Stitch the side border strip to the accent border, stitching ⅛" from the *previous seam line and extension line,* not from the outside edges you normally follow. Press the seam flat, then away from the center of the project. Add the remaining side strip and trim the ends even with the top and bottom. When finished, look at your work. Now you can see where the sewing lines run parallel only an ⅛" apart, and your seam allowance to the right is ⅜" wide, not the normal ¼". If this bothers you, now is the time to trim.

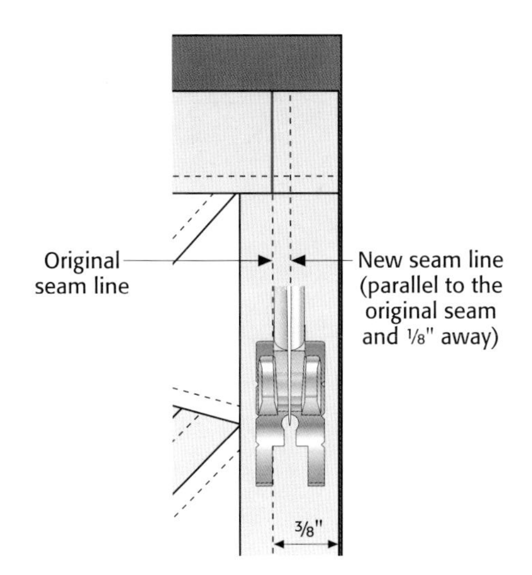

8. After the side borders have been applied, turn the block to the wrong side and draw in the new extension lines for the top and bottom strips.

9. Add the top and bottom strips; trim the ends even with the sides. Turn your work over and look at the right side. Look at that accurate, wonderful, ⅛" border. Wow!

DON'T BE CONCERNED with how accurate or even the seam allowances are on the back. Concentrate on how even the border appears on the front and how dramatic it looks.

STEP 5: ADD REMAINING BORDERS

Continue in this manner with any remaining borders. Remember to use a regular ¼" seam allowance when adding more accent borders. You only use the ⅛" sewing guide when adding the border following the accent border.

Some of the quilts are finished with a mitered outer border. For directions on applying mitered borders, see "Making Borders with Mitered Corners" on page 20.

Making Borders with Mitered Corners

1. Cut the border strips as indicated in the cutting directions for each quilt.
2. On the quilt, mark the center of each side of the quilt top. Mark the ¼" seam intersections on the 4 quilt corners.

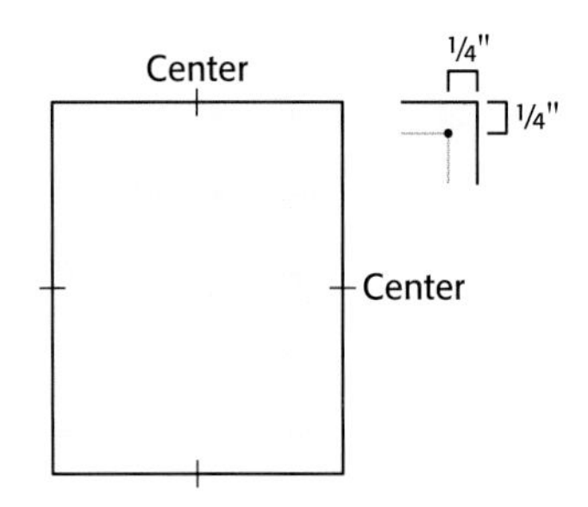

3. Mark the center of each border strip and ¼" in from where the corners of the quilt will be.

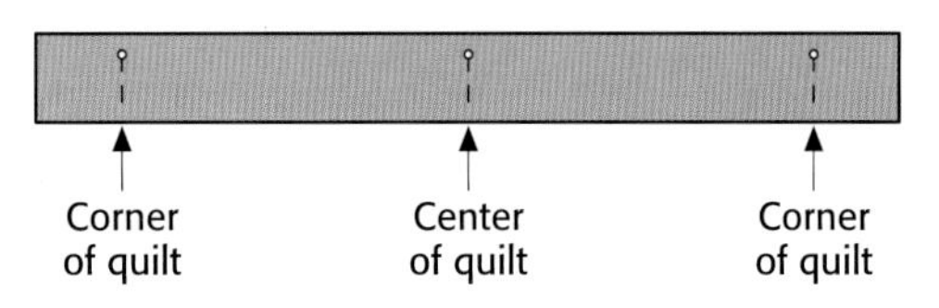

4. With right sides together, pin the side border strips to the quilt sides, matching center and corner marks. Stitch from corner mark to corner mark. Press the seam allowances toward the border. Repeat for the top and bottom borders, making sure the stitching lines meet exactly at the corners.

Quilt top

5. With right sides together, fold the quilt diagonally so that the border strips are aligned. Using a ruler with a 45° angle, draw a line on the wrong side of the border strip from the corner mark to the outside edge as shown.

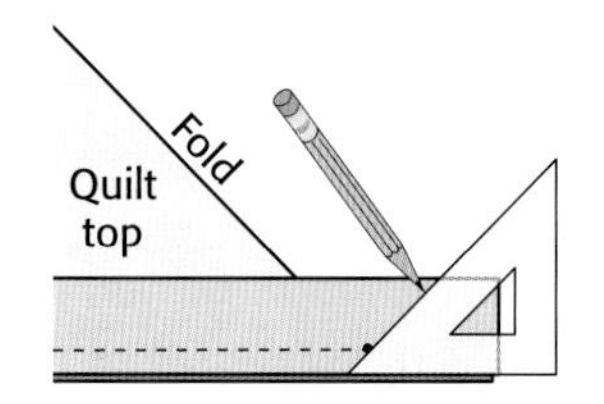

6. Pin the borders together and stitch on the drawn line. Open out the top and make sure the seam is flat and accurate before trimming the seam allowances. Press the seam open. Repeat for the remaining corners.

Finishing Touches

THE BLOCKS ARE sewn, the sashing and borders are attached, and the foundation paper has been removed. The end of the project is now within sight. Only the finishing touches remain. Don't stop now, but don't rush either. These final touches often make the quilt. Take the time to do them right. Give them the focus, the energy, and the attention they deserve.

Embellishing

Adding basic embroidery lines, buttons, and beads can enhance the overall appearance of your Needles and Notions blocks. These details complete the imagery and detail of the particular sewing notions, making them more realistic looking while adding texture and dimension to the surface of your quilt. Suddenly the quilt takes on a more fun and whimsical appeal, drawing the viewer in for a more careful study and examination and perhaps even a touch. Add embroidery after assembling the quilt top; add buttons and beads after quilting.

Embroidery

The basic stitch, known as an outline or stem stitch, is used to outline areas and to add the detail lines to the measurement marks of the tape measure, the thread through the needle, the pins in the pincushion, and the needle of the sewing machine.

To stem stitch, use these steps:

1. On your pieced block, lightly draw the desired design lines with a water-soluble marker or a pencil.
2. Cut off an 18" length of embroidery thread or floss in the desired color. Separate the 6 strands into 2-strand lengths.
3. Thread the needle with a 2-strand length and knot the end.
4. Insert the needle. As you begin, bury the knot, if possible, behind some darker fabric, or else gently weave the end into the stitches as you work.
5. Bring the thread to the front of the fabric at point A. Insert the needle at point B, and then come out at point C. Repeat to the end of the drawn line, spacing the stitches evenly. Bury the thread end by reweaving it into the stitching on the fabric wrong side.

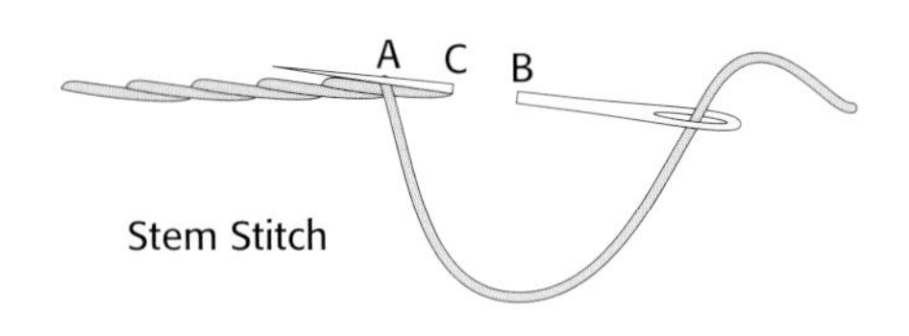

THESE FABRIC PIECES and blocks are delicate. Try not to stretch your blocks or pull the embroidery thread too tight as you stitch.

Buttons

Buttons come in all sizes, shapes, colors, and materials: wooden, ceramic, plastic, metal, pearl, etc. They are added to the blocks after the quilt is quilted to bring texture and dimension to the surface. Use your own imagination and creativity to search out special places and ways to let button embellishments enhance your quilt.

The following are some placement and attachment suggestions:

- Add a button to the joint or pivot point of the scissors.
- Stack two sizes of buttons on top of each other to depict the blade and screw of the rotary cutter.
- "Fill" your button jar with all kinds of buttons. Consider adding some charms and other found treasures for interest and surprise.
- Cluster the buttons so that they lie on top of one another or lap over each other.
- Leave the strands of the threads hanging loose on the right side for added textural appeal.
- Sew buttons to your sashing and borders. Bring in extra color with tiny buttons sewn at the corners of each sashing square.
- Sew tiny buttons on "Sewing Room Sue's" dress front.

Beads

Beads, like buttons, come in a wide variety of shapes, sizes, colors, and materials and should be added after the quilt has been quilted. They vary widely in price, but when used appropriately, they add special detail and sparkle.

In these blocks, beads represent the heads of the sewing pins and the tip of the seam ripper, but do not be limited to these places. Try adding beadwork elsewhere to bring more depth and interest to your work.

Here are some useful hints for bead embellishment:

- Use a beading needle, which is longer and thinner than a traditional needle and has a longer eye for easier threading. The needle size should be smaller than the bead size.

- Use all-purpose mercerized cotton sewing thread in a color that most nearly matches the beads. Using a closely matching color will help minimize distractions.
- Standard seed beads are used on these quilts. Such beads are available in most hobby shops and chain stores.
- Sew the beads on one at a time, stitching through all three layers of the quilt.
- When attaching a bead, go through the bead at least twice. This will cause the bead to stand up and be more visible.

Basting

The time has come when the three layers—quilt top, batting, and backing—need to be temporarily bound together by basting. Well-done basting sets the stage for trouble-free quilting.

1. Prewash the backing fabric and batting, if needed or desired. Check the batting manufacturer's instructions, as well.
2. Cut the backing fabric and batting 4" to 6" larger than the pieced top. This allows for some drawing up of the top as you quilt or for some shifting and movement of the top.
3. Build the layers from the bottom up. First, place the backing fabric right side down on the table or other flat work surface. Secure it with masking tape in several places along the edges. This helps to keep the fabric smooth and taut. Second, place the batting on top of the secured backing. It, too, can be secured by the masking tape, if needed. With your hands, smooth it out from the center. Third, center the pieced top, right side up, onto the batting and backing. Smooth it out.
4. Baste the layers together, using 1 of the methods and patterns described in "Basting Methods and Patterns" on page 23.

Quilting

When basting has been completed, you are ready to quilt. You may have many questions about this process. Do I hand quilt or machine quilt? What design? Simple lines or complicated patterns? How much? The questions are many, but you must decide.

Perhaps it would help to keep quilting's twofold purpose in mind: 1) to add enough quilting to permanently bond the layers, and 2) to enhance the piecework and bring dimension and depth to the quilt top.

Paper-foundation-pieced projects often have the added disadvantage of many, many seam allowances, which can cause hand-quilting difficulties. Machine quilting, using a nylon monofilament thread, is much easier.

The following five quilting suggestions are provided as just that: suggestions. They are ways of quilting that have worked well on the quilts pictured in this book. They work effectively individually and in combination with each other. Obviously, this is not an exhaustive list of the quilting possibilities, but perhaps it is enough to get your brain and quilting started. Be bold! Do your own thing! But remember these two things: It is not a quilt until it is quilted, and keep it simple. (For more information about machine quilting, refer to *Machine Quilting Made Easy,* That Patchwork Place.)

- In-the-ditch quilting. Within the blocks, identify individual parts of each sewing notion and then carefully quilt in the seam lines around those areas. For instance, the cup and saucer consists of four basic parts: the table, the saucer, the cup, and the inside of the cup. Each of these parts can be outlined with quilting, treating each as a complete unit, regardless of how many pieces are actually within that part.

In-the-ditch quilting

Basting Methods and Patterns

Several methods of basting exist. You may use safety pins, tacks, thread, or even straight pins. Every quilter has a preference as to which method to use, and the preference may change depending upon the size of the quilt, the time available, and whether she wants to hand or machine quilt.

Generally, if you plan on machine quilting, tack the layers together with size 0 or 1 safety pins or with a QuilTak tacking gun. Either of these methods allows you to remove the pins or tacks as you approach them with your machine needle. On a small wall hanging, you even can use straight pins for basting.

If you are hand quilting, you may wish to thread-baste your layers together.

Whatever method you choose, pin or baste from the center out so that all puckers or wrinkles are smoothed and eased out to the edges.

Three frequently used patterns for basting are grid lines or rows, diagonal lines, and radiating spokes of a wheel. Simple random placement is another option.

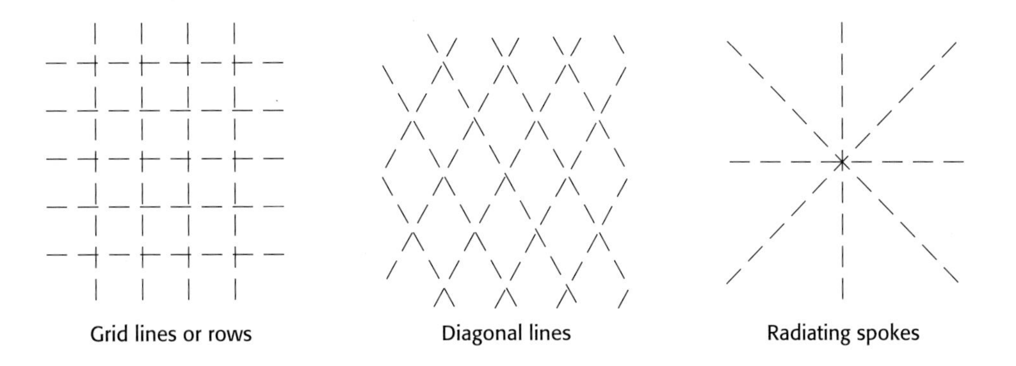

Grid lines or rows — Diagonal lines — Radiating spokes

Baste or pin every 3" to 4". It is better to have too much basting than too little. Keep in mind that the purpose is to prevent the layers from shifting any more than necessary and to prevent puckers and folds from developing in the backing as you quilt.

These blocks are small enough that you may choose not to quilt the backgrounds at all, but rather to add simple in-the-ditch quilting around the outer perimeter. For examples of in-the-ditch quilting, refer to any of the photos of the Needles and Notions blocks, as well as "Tutti-Frutti" (page 66) and "Calypso—Flip 'n' Sew!" (page 68).

- Meandering or stipple quilting. Alternately, you can quilt the block backgrounds with an allover meandering, or stippling, stitch. This gives the background a bubbly texture that can be very appealing, both to the eye and to the touch. However, it does require that you move into the realm of free-motion quilting. It takes some practice, but it is great for adding texture and quickly covering background areas. For examples, see "Country Sampler" (page 71) and "Under the Ivy" (page 74).

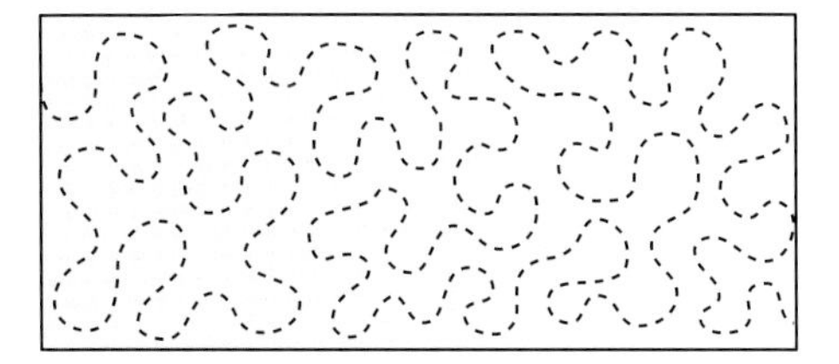

Meandering or stipple quilting

- Channel quilting. After quilting in the ditch of the borders, add additional lines of parallel stitching within the borders. Repeat the lines several times to create a soft ridge effect. For examples of channel-quilted borders, see "Tutti-Frutti" (page 66) and "Country Sampler" (page 71).
- Follow the printed design. Consider letting your fabric make the quilting decisions for you. If the border fabric has a design, carefully machine stitch around the shapes and designs printed on the fabric. Once again, however, this does call for some free-motion quilting. The borders in "Under the Ivy" (page 74) and "Sue—At the Head of the (Sewing) Class" (page 77) are examples of following the printed design.
- Free-floating designs using stencils. Finally, you could easily quilt in particular patterns and shapes that reflect some design already present in the quilt. The border print used in "Under the Ivy" (page 74) left large, open background areas under the scalloped vines. These areas looked too bare and plain left unquilted, so a three-leaf pattern was designed that fit into the open area. It was traced onto the top using a plastic stencil of that design and then quilted. The design repeated what was already in the quilt and effectively filled in the space.

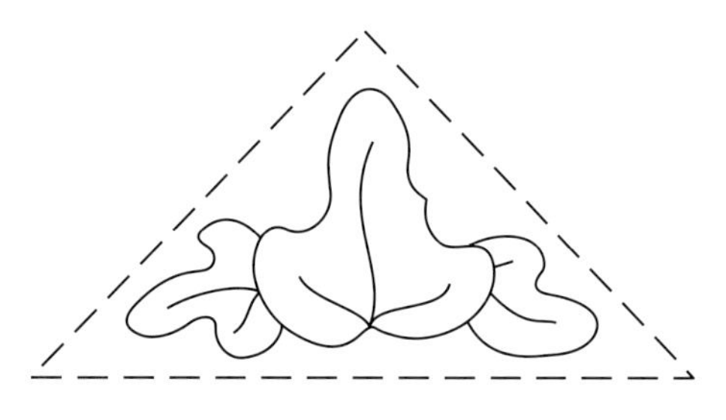

Attaching a Rod Pocket

There are many ways to hang your quilts. You need a sleeve of some type that allows the insertion of a rod or dowel at the quilt top; thus the name *rod pocket.* By using a rod pocket, you allow the rod or dowel to be inserted without touching, staining, or otherwise damaging the back of your quilt.

Follow these steps to make a rod pocket:

1. Measure the width of your quilt at the top and subtract 2". Cut a fabric strip to that length and 5" to 9" wide, depending upon the rod you plan to use for hanging. If needed, cut more than 1 strip and sew the ends together to create the desired length.
2. Press under each end ¼". Press under ¼" again and stitch ⅛" from the first folded edge.

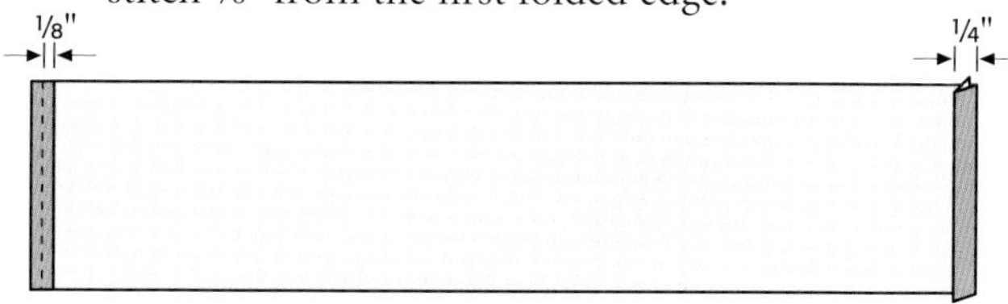

3. Fold the strip in half lengthwise, wrong sides together. Pin it together at the ends and at several points in between. Press.

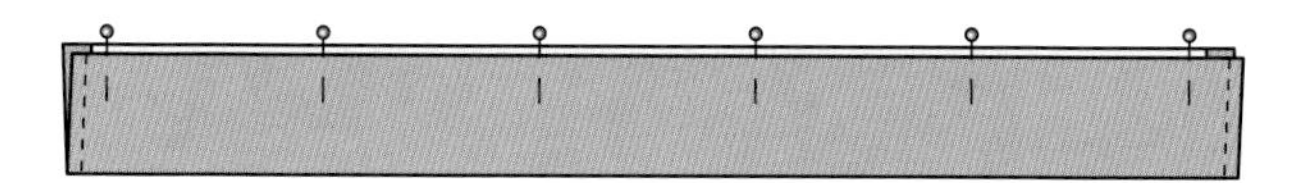

4. Center the rod pocket on the back of the quilt at the upper edge, aligning raw edges; pin in place. As you add the binding to the upper edge of the quilt, you will automatically attach the rod pocket.
5. After you apply the binding, hand hemstitch the bottom edge of the rod pocket to the quilt back. Be sure to catch only the backing and batting and leave the ends of the sleeve open, sewing only the bottom layer of the rod pocket to the quilt.

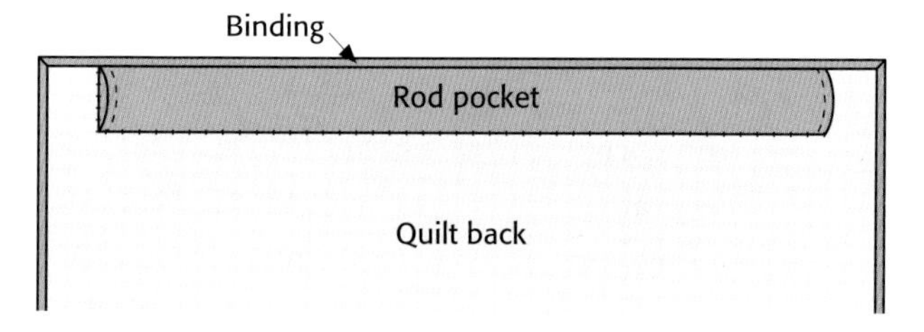

Binding

After the quilt is quilted, it is time to bind the outer edges. This method allows you to hide the place where the binding ends meet. It looks just like the rest of the binding and does not cause a bulky place along the outer edge of the quilt.

1. Square up the quilt layers by trimming the excess batting and backing even with the top.
2. Using your rotary-cutting equipment, cut enough 2"-wide strips to go around the quilt, with enough

extra for corner turns and final joining. Join the strips with diagonal seams into 1 long continuous binding strip.

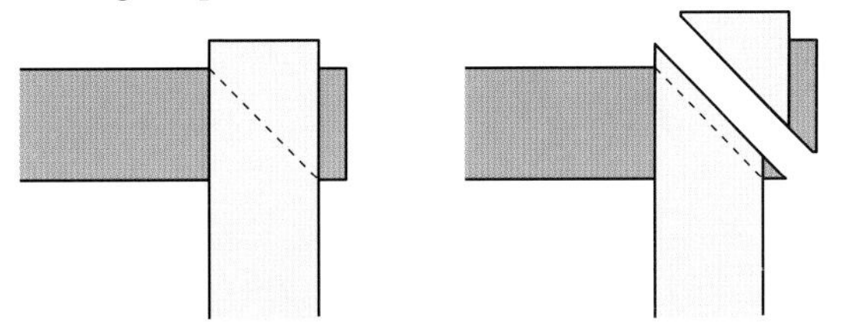

3. Press the binding in half lengthwise, wrong sides and raw edges together.

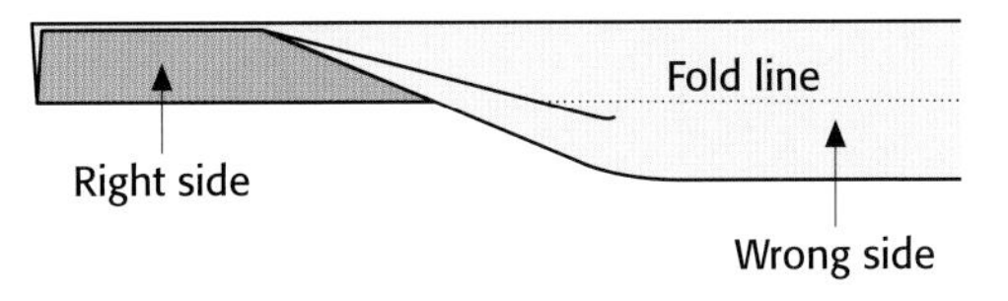

4. Beginning on one side and leaving an 8" tail at the beginning, place the binding on the quilt top, aligning the binding raw edges with the quilt raw edge. Using a ¼" seam allowance, stitch the binding to the quilt top, backstitching at the beginning and stopping ¼" from the corner; backstitch and remove the quilt from the machine.

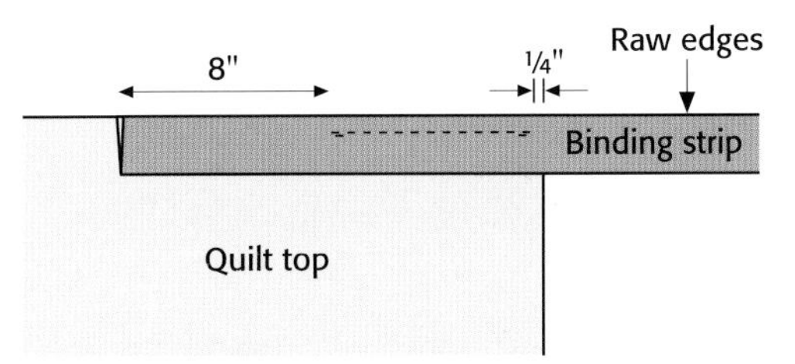

5. With the corner directly in front of you, fold the binding straight up, creating a 45° angle. Then fold the binding straight down, with the fold even with the edges of the quilt. The raw edges of the binding are now even with the next side.

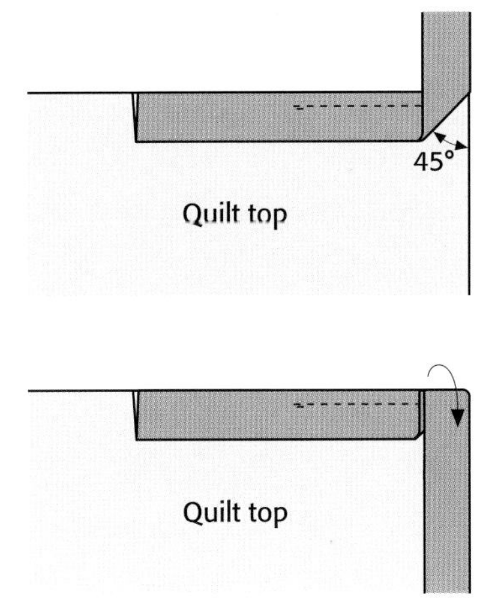

6. Begin stitching just off the fabric at the corner. The new seam is now perpendicular to the previous stitched line. Continue until you are ¼" from the next corner and repeat step 5. Repeat for all 4 corners of the quilt, stopping 5" to 10" from where you originally began stitching. Backstitch.

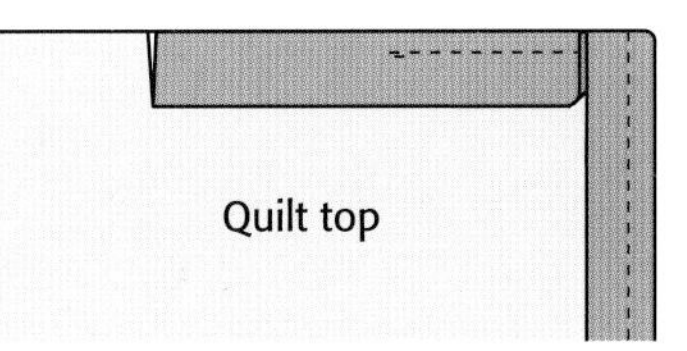

7. Remove the quilt from the machine and leave an 8"-long tail of binding. Lay the quilt flat on the ironing board and carefully fold the 2 tails together at the center. Press, creating an easily seen crease line.

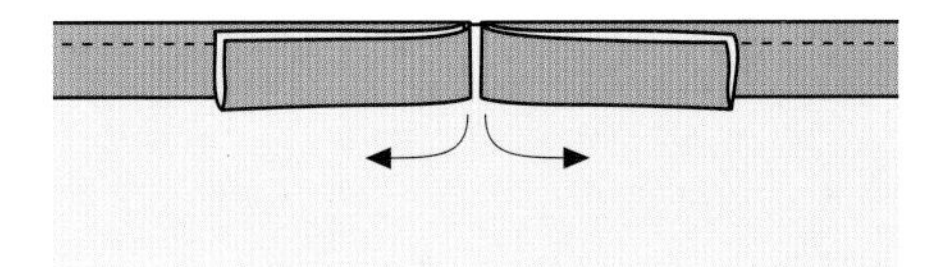

8. Unfold the strip ends. Lay 1 flat, with the right side up. Lay the other, right side down, over it, matching the crease points on the edges. Carefully draw a diagonal line through the point where the fold lines meet. Stitch through the marked line.

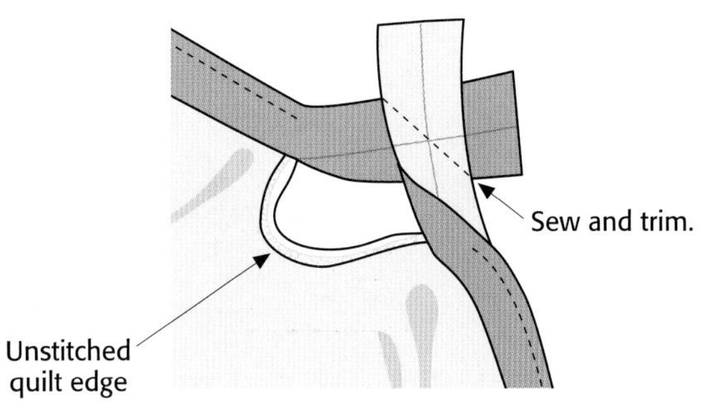

9. Check to make sure the newly attached binding is the correct length and closes the gap. If so, trim the tails off ¼" from the seam. Finger-press the seam allowance open. Refold the binding and finish sewing the binding between the beginning and ending points.

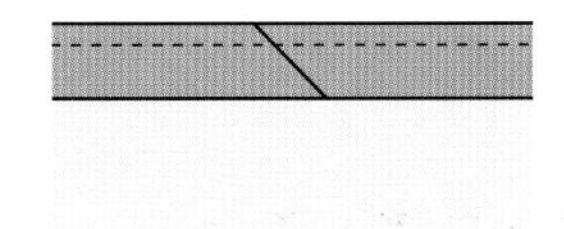

10. Gently bring the binding from the front of the quilt to the back and pin it in place. The binding should easily fold over the seam allowance and just cover the stitching line. Using a thread color that matches the binding, whipstitch the folded edge of the binding to the back of the quilt, being careful that your stitches do not go through to the front of the quilt. As you reach the corners, gently pull the binding straight out. With your thumbnail in the corner, fold over the unstitched binding edge, creating a mitered corner. Secure it with stitching. Do this for all the corners of the quilt.

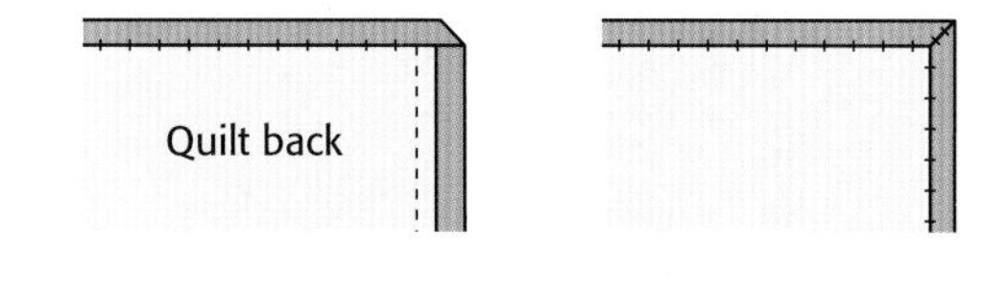

Labeling

Labeling your quilts is really an important final touch because it defines your quilts historically. Who will know in the future who made this quilt and the details about it if you do not sign it?

Signature labels can be very simple, with merely your name and date. Or they can contain quite elaborate stories of your quilt with additional information, such as why it was made, for whom, special bits of information about particular fabric choices or special buttons or embellishments that were added, special techniques used, if any, and much more. Do not disappoint and frustrate some quilt lover or collector who, fifty years from now, wants to know more about the quilt that she is considering purchasing. Write it down and place it on the back of the quilt.

Now we truly know what this statement means: "To quilt is human, to finish is divine." It is a divine feeling! And we just can't wait to start the process over again! Stand up and take a bow! You deserve it! Enjoy it!

Synergism, or 2 + 2 > 4

In conclusion, slow down and truly savor the wonder and magic of what we do as quilters. Do not forget that the quilting walk or journey calls for time to reflect; time to truly touch and feel our work as we go along; time to take in our designs and color choices, workmanship, and effort. As sewers and quilters, our quilts are so much more than simply fabric and thread. This is a reference to the concept of synergy: two plus two can equal more than four. The whole is more than simply a sum of the parts.

When we sew and quilt, the end products of our effort are so much more than simply the fabric we buy, the tools we use, or the time we spend. Our quilts truly represent and reflect our lives: our triumphs and joys, our heartaches and pain, our laughter and tears, our memories and goals. All of these, the good and the bad, are stitched into our quilts and wall hangings. Our quilts have become us, and we are our quilts! That is a pretty awesome concept.

As you use these blocks and patterns, may your sewing walk be blessed with quilt projects that speak volumes about you and two of your life's pleasures—sewing and quilting!

I'm glad you stopped along the way. Sit a spell and stay awhile. Enjoy the journey!

THE BLOCKS

THE QUILTS SHOWN *in this book feature twelve different Needles and Notions paper-foundation-pieced blocks. They each represent a very important piece of equipment to those of us who enjoy sewing and quilting. The complete set includes a button jar, cup and saucer, iron, needle, pincushion, rotary cutter, pair of scissors, seam ripper, sewing machine, spools of thread, tape measure, and thimble. In addition, I have included a Sewing Room Sue paper-foundation-pieced block to accent the charm of these special blocks. This block was deliberately designed to be larger than necessary so it could be trimmed to fit into a variety of settings with the Needles and Notions blocks.*

The block patterns provided in the book are for both the 4" and 6" blocks. The sewing order is the same regardless of size, and the fabric requirements vary little, but the difference in piecing difficulty can be evident. For this reason, the beginning paper piecer should start with the 6" size. Develop your skill and technique, then move to the smaller 4" blocks.

Also, there is some difference in piecing difficulty from block to block. The more intricate notions have more parts and require a bit more piecing finesse (i.e., the tape measure or the thimble), while other blocks are relatively easy, regardless of size (i.e., the scissors or the rotary cutter). Again, build on your skills, and start with easier blocks. Refer to "Block Embellishment Guides" on pages 55–57 to add the embellishments shown on the blocks indicated.

BUTTON JAR

QUILTERS DON'T *do buttons! (At least not the ones on our spouse's shirts.) But, wow, do we ever love to collect them, use them for embellishment, or just keep them in old mason jars! How satisfying it is to dip our hand into a large jar of buttons and let them roll over our fingers!*

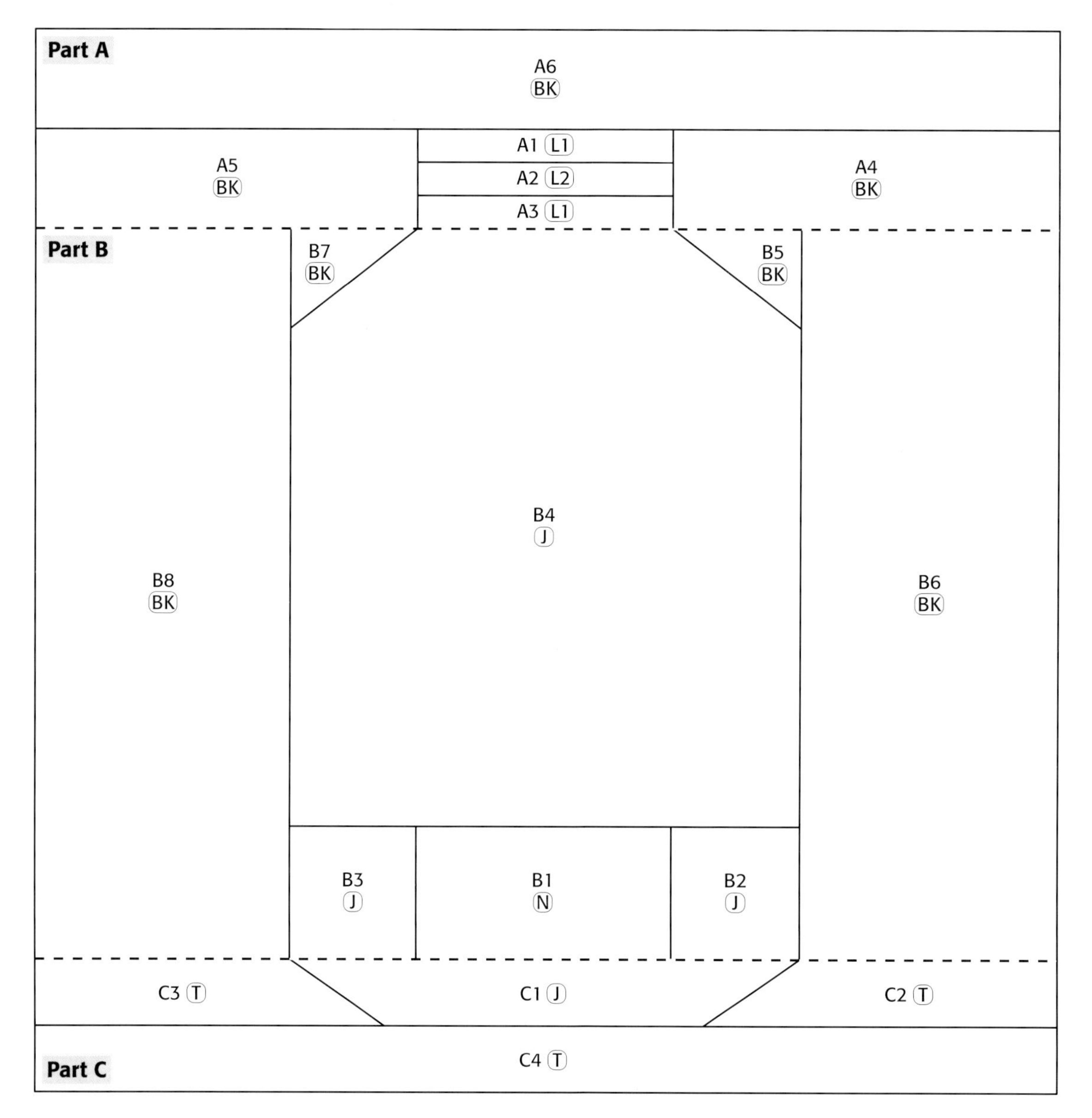

Foundation Pattern

Fabric Key

BK–Background

J–Jar

L1–Lid #1 (Darker)

L2–Lid #2 (Lighter)

N–Neutral for Buttons Label

T–Table

Sewing Order

Part A: 1–6

Part B: 1–8

Join A to B (AB)

Part C: 1–4

Join AB to C (ABC)

Block Embellishment Guide

See page 56.

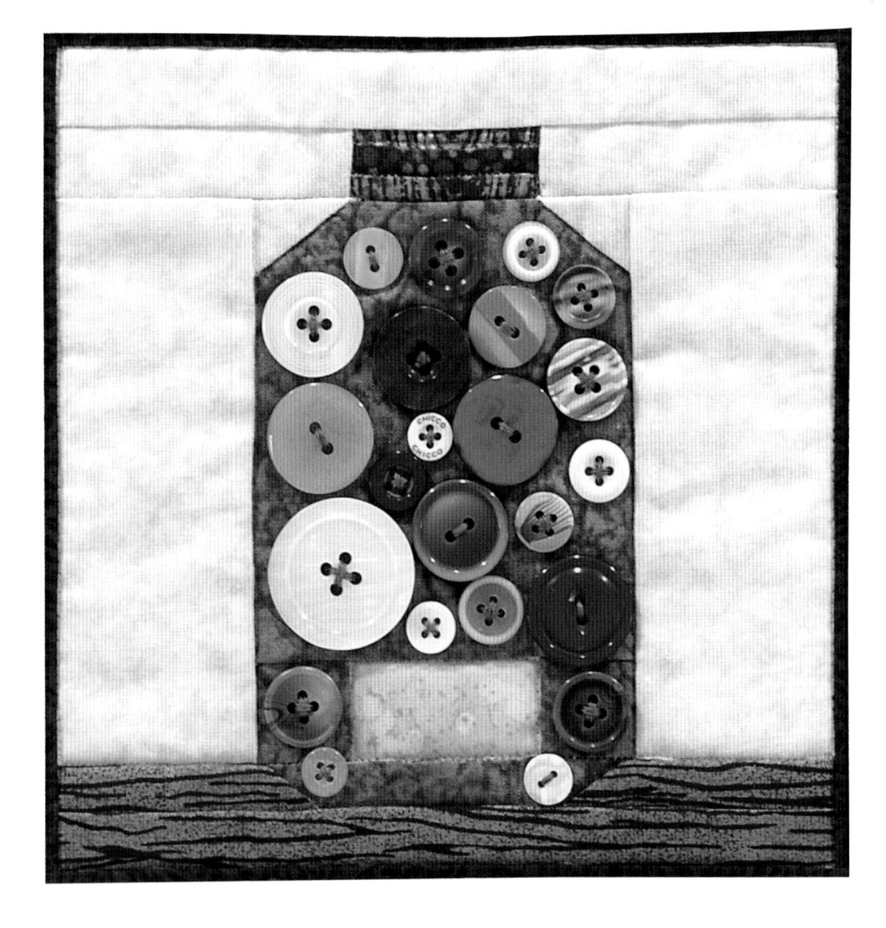

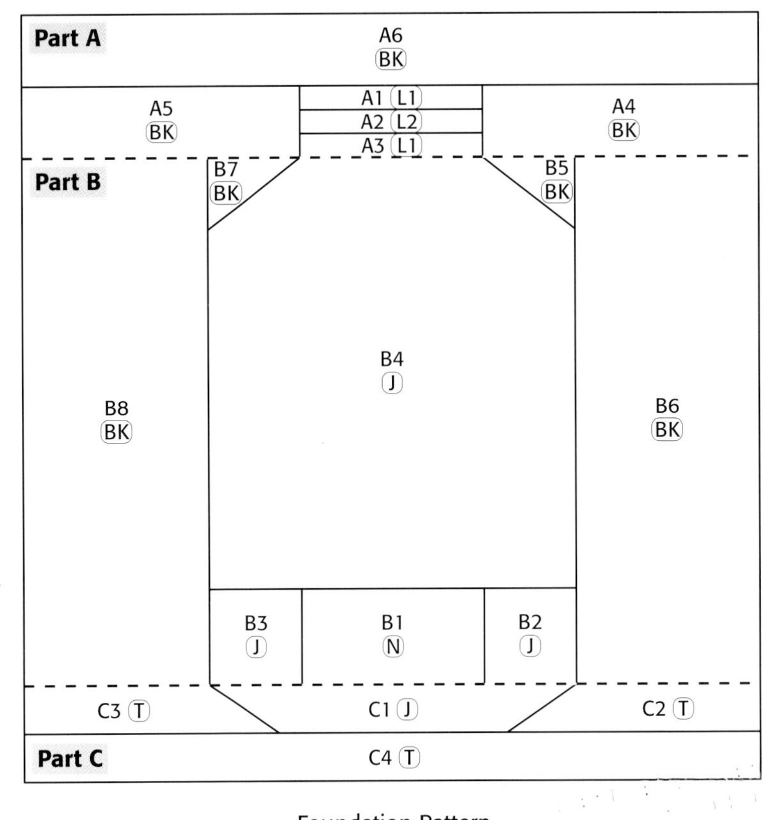

Foundation Pattern

CUP AND SAUCER

DRINK UP! *What quilter can work without a cup of coffee or tea beside her? It is the companion to our solitude that refreshes and gives us that moment to reflect on our workmanship, the designs, and the thoughts behind so many of our quilts.*

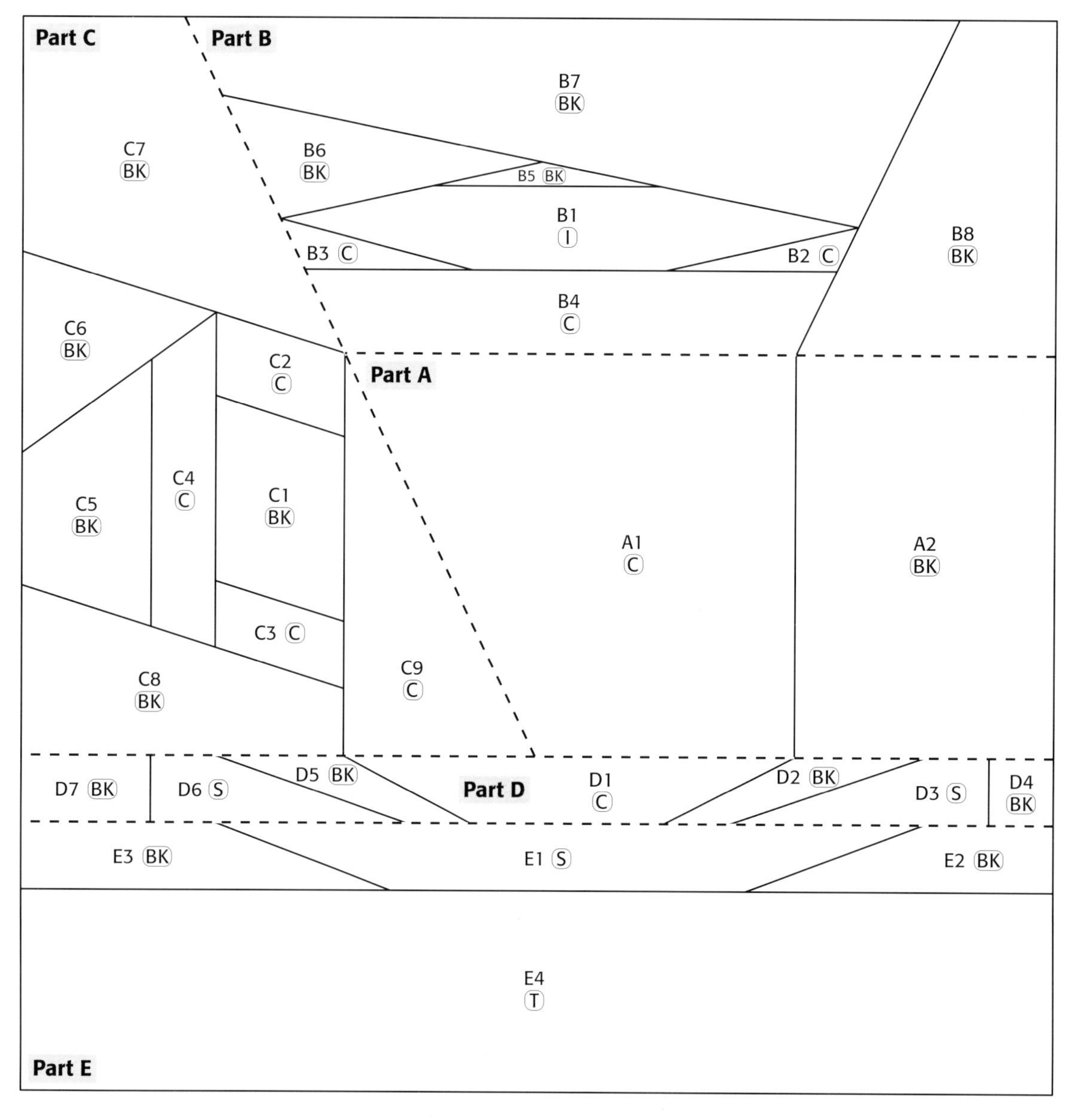

Foundation Pattern

Fabric Key

BK–Background
C–Cup
I–Inside of Cup
S–Saucer
T–Tabletop

Sewing Order

Part A: 1–2
Part B: 1–8
Join A to B (AB)
Part C: 1–9
Join AB to C (ABC)
Part D: 1–7
Join ABC to D (ABCD)
Part E: 1–4
Join ABCD to E (ABCDE)

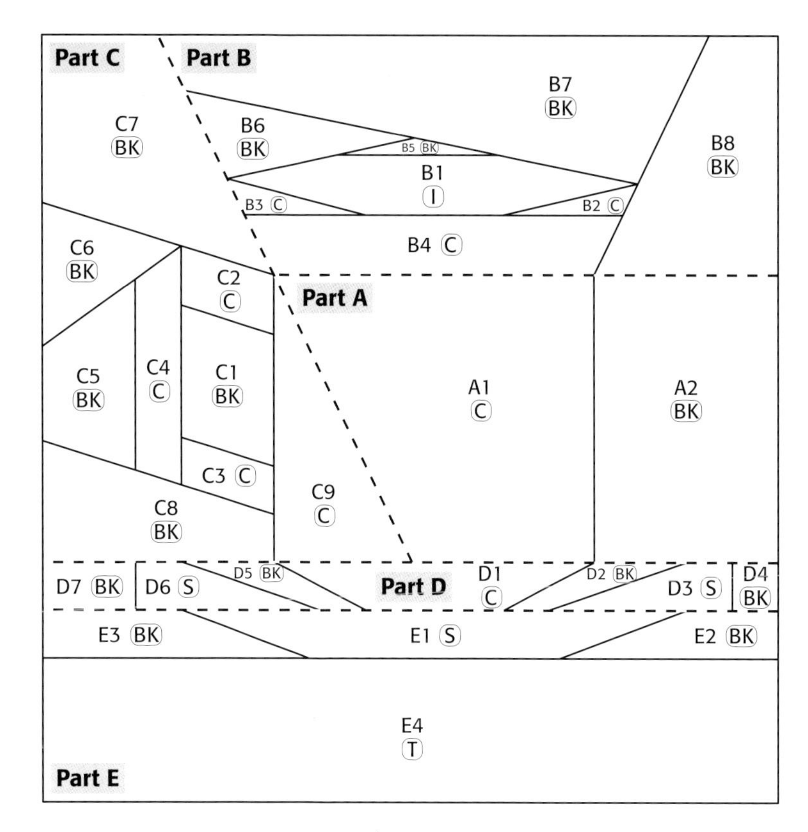

Foundation Pattern

IRON

We quilters *iron every day—and love it! But it is not our laundry we are doing! It is so much more fun to iron our luscious fabrics. What a wonderful way to get really up close and personal with their prints and colors and textures.*

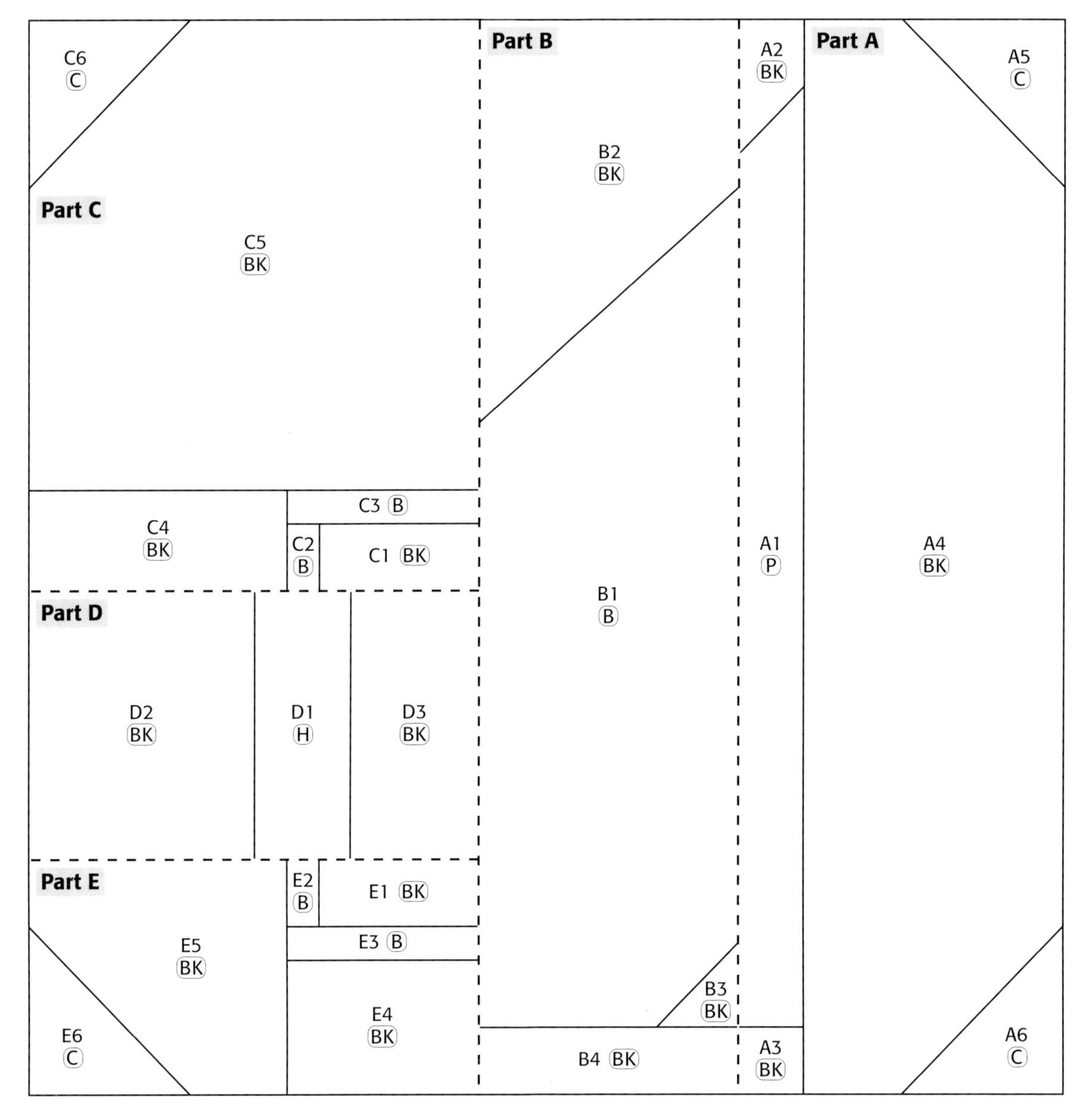

Foundation Pattern

Fabric Key

BK–Background
B–Body
C–Corners
H–Handle
P–Plate

Sewing Order

Part A: 1–6
Part B: 1–4
Join A to B (AB)
Part C: 1–6
Part D: 1–3
Join C to D (CD)
Part E: 1–6
Join CD to E (CDE)
Join AB to CDE (ABCDE)

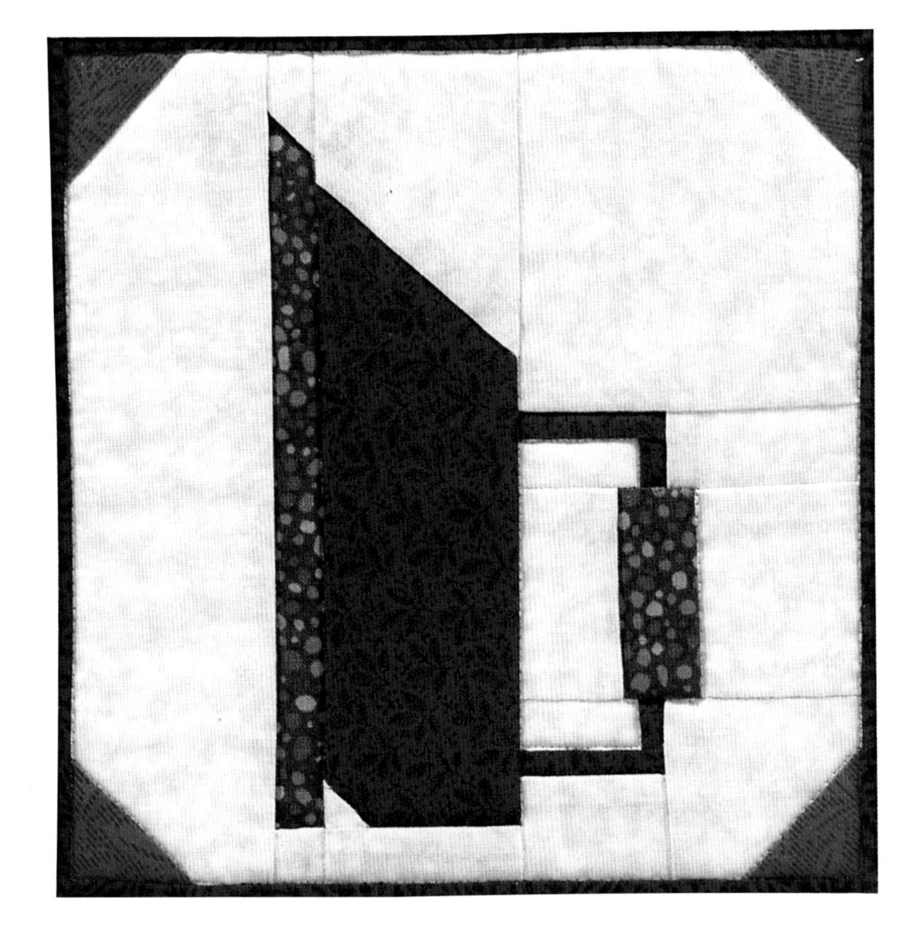

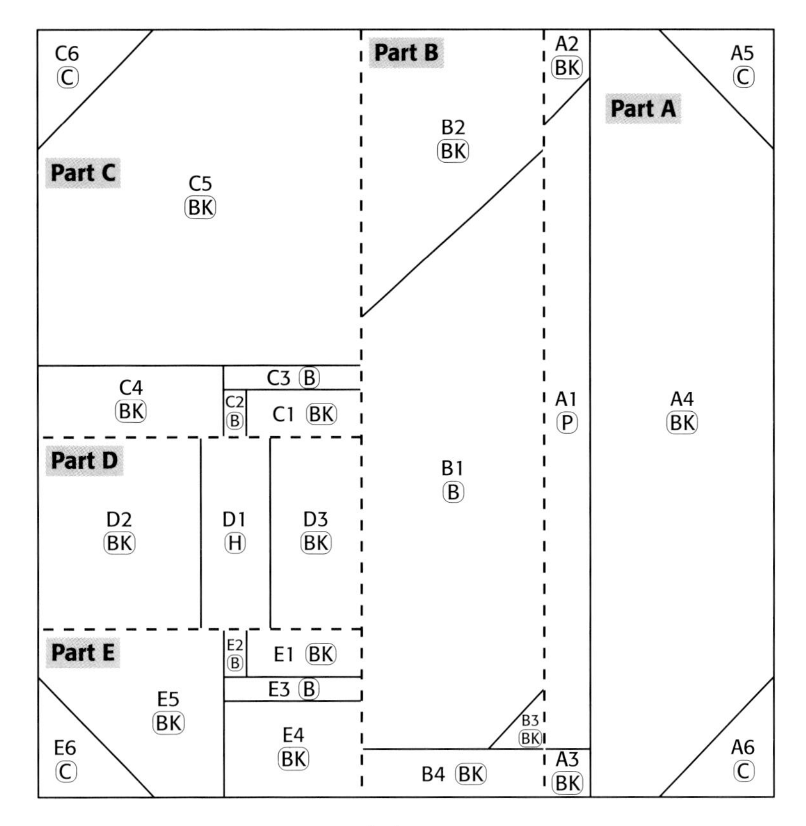

Foundation Pattern

NEEDLE

OOPS, I LEFT *my needle in the arm of my favorite chair in the living room, and now it is gone! Where, oh, where can my lost needle be? Fear not; it will turn up—with luck, before some family member steps on it!*

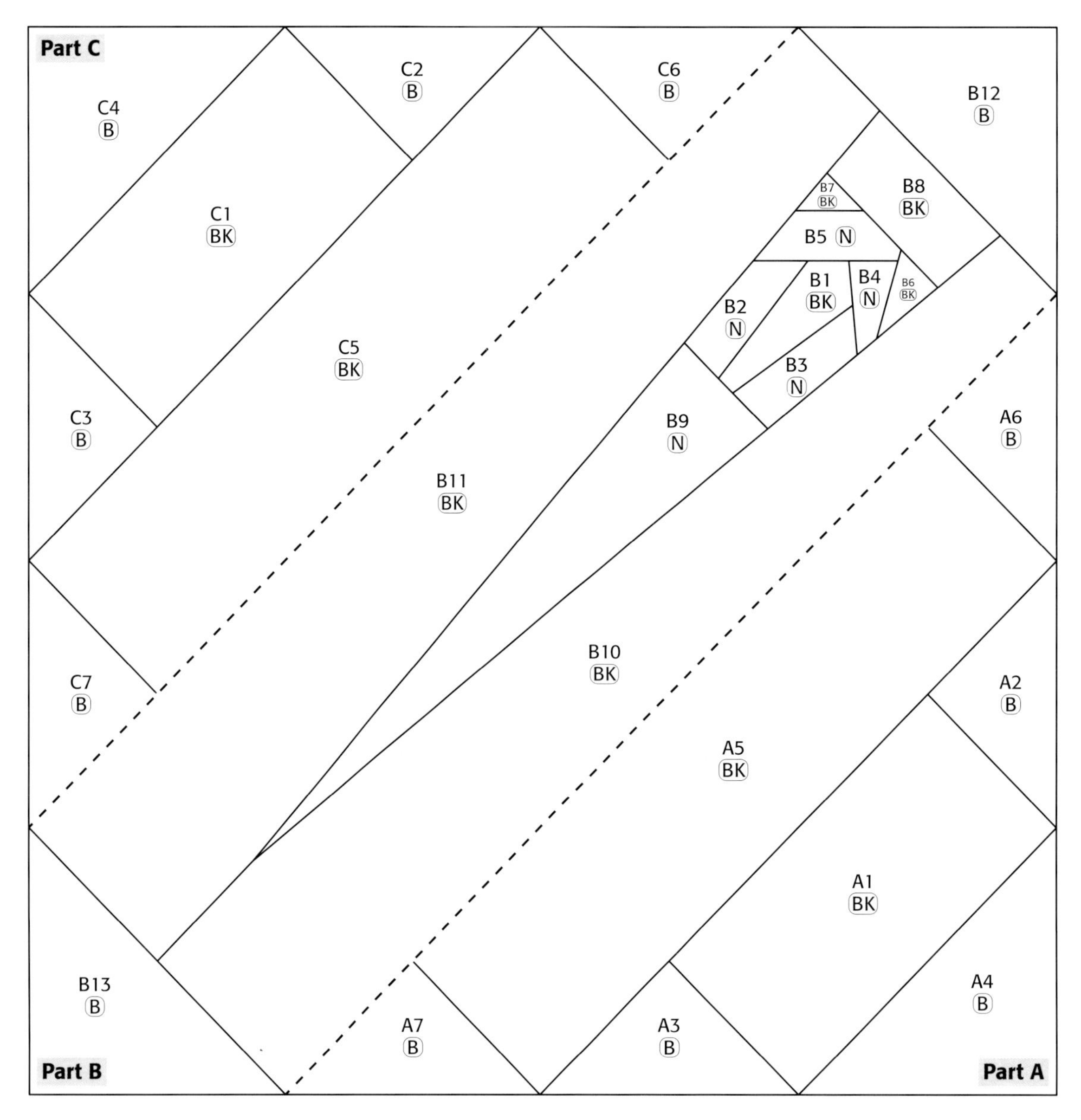

Foundation Pattern

Fabric Key

BK–Background

B–Border

N–Needle

Sewing Order

Part A: 1–7

Part B: 1–13

Join A to B (AB)

Part C: 1–7

Join AB to C (ABC)

Block Embellishment Guide

See page 55.

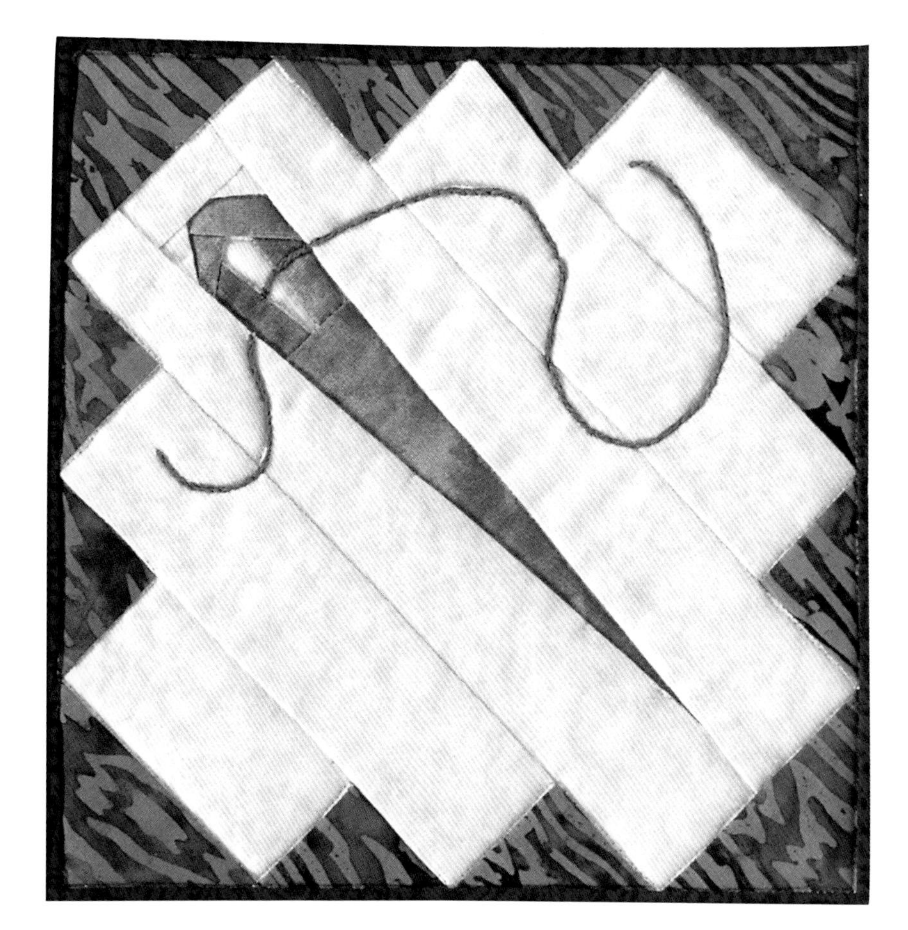

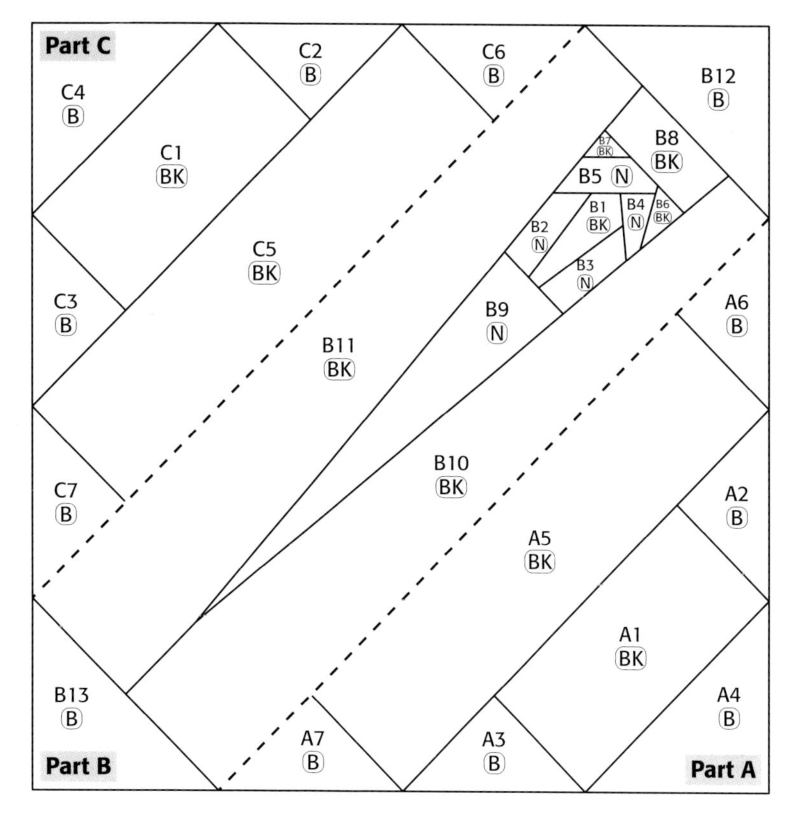

Foundation Pattern

PINCUSHION

*B*E THEY STRAWBERRY *red and full of sawdust or beautiful lamb's wool dyed glorious colors, pincushions still serve the same function: to maintain our needles and pins and keep sharp points safely tucked away.*

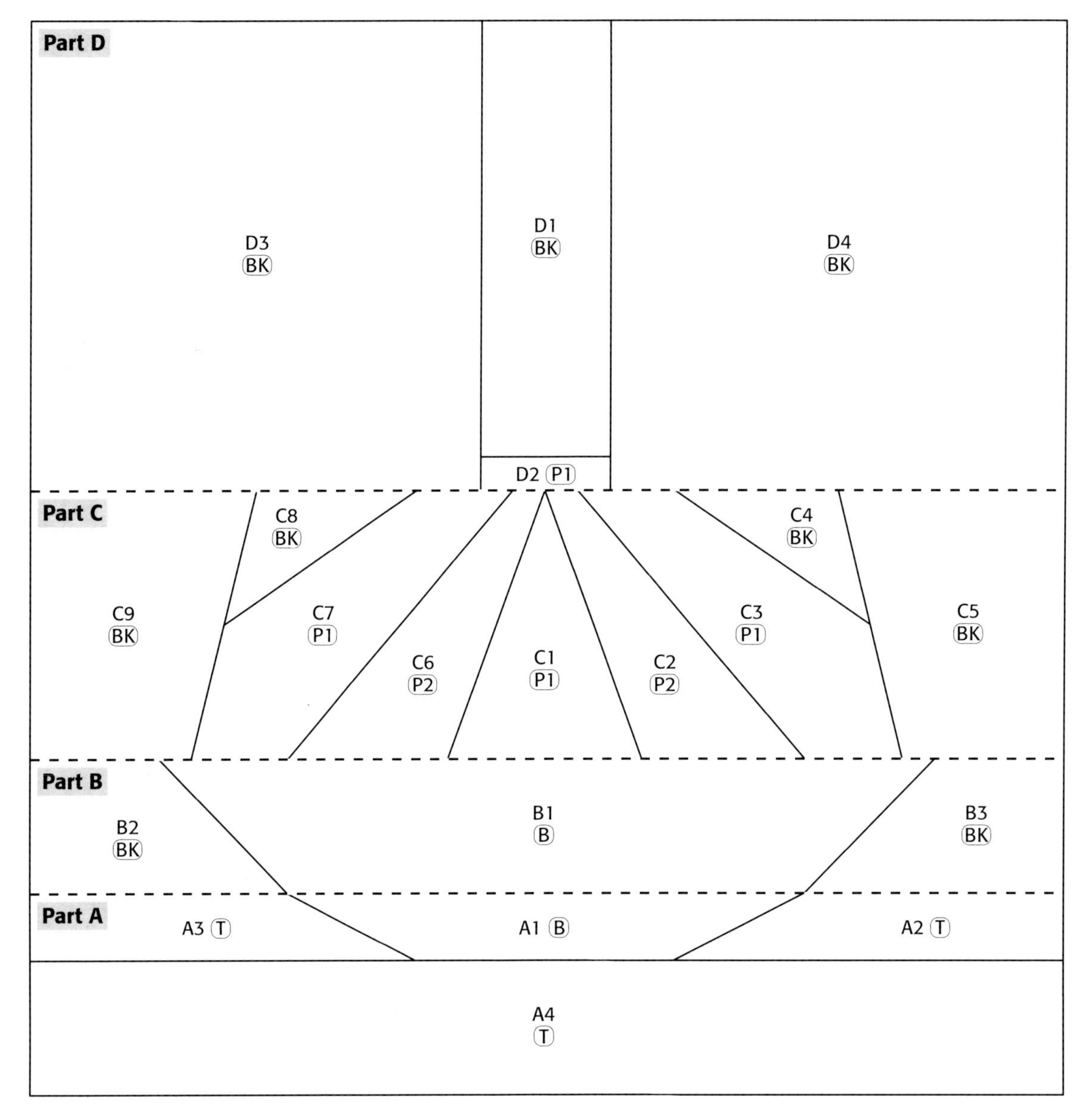

Foundation Pattern

Fabric Key

BK–Background

B–Basket

P1–Pincushion 1

P2–Pincushion 2

T–Table

Sewing Order

Part A: 1–4

Part B: 1–3

Join A to B (AB)

Part C: 1–9

Join AB to C (ABC)

Part D: 1–4

Join ABC to D (ABCD)

Block Embellishment Guide

See page 57.

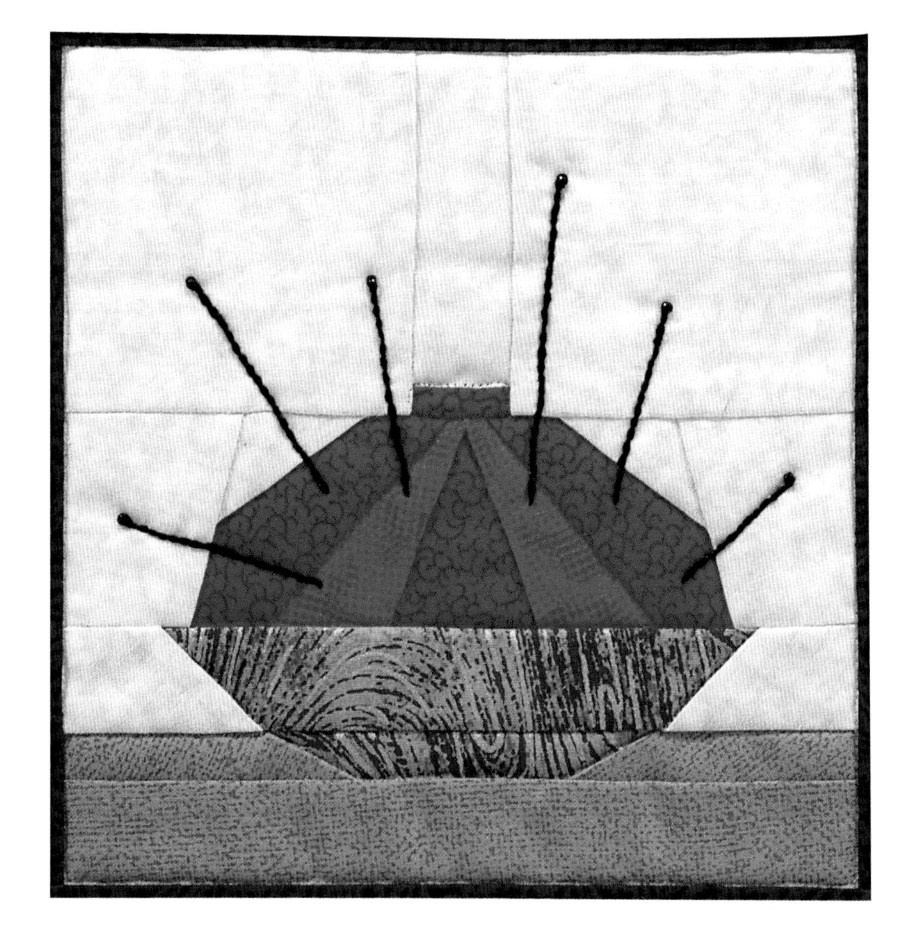

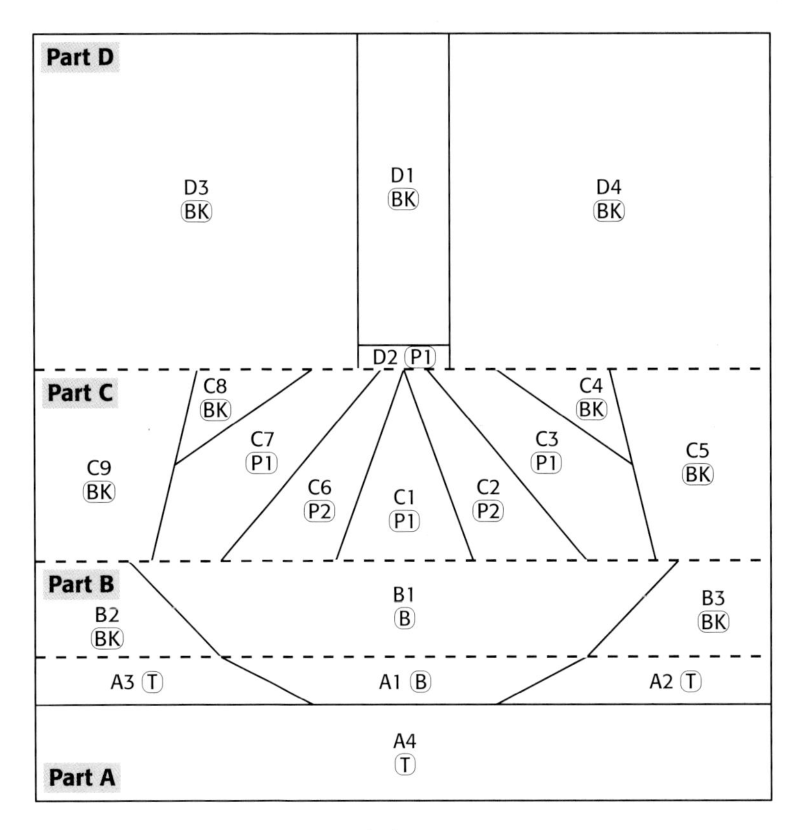

Foundation Pattern

ROTARY CUTTER

*W*HO CAN LIVE *without this tool anymore? It may look like a pizza cutter, but we all know it leads to accurate cuts in a short amount of time.*

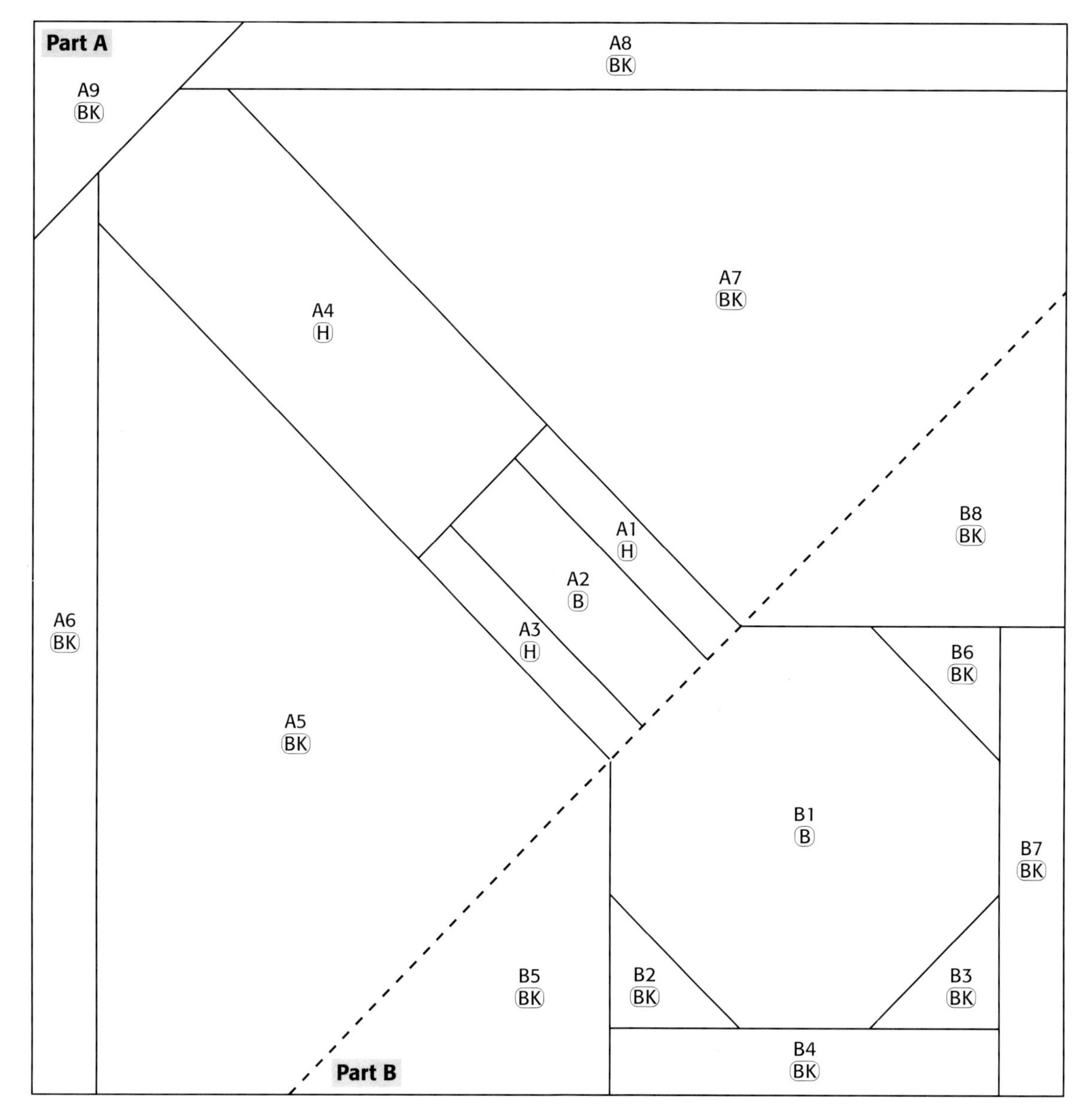

Foundation Pattern

Fabric Key

BK–Background

B–Blade

H–Handle

Sewing Order

Part A: 1–9

Part B: 1–8

Join A to B (AB)

Block Embellishment Guide

See page 55.

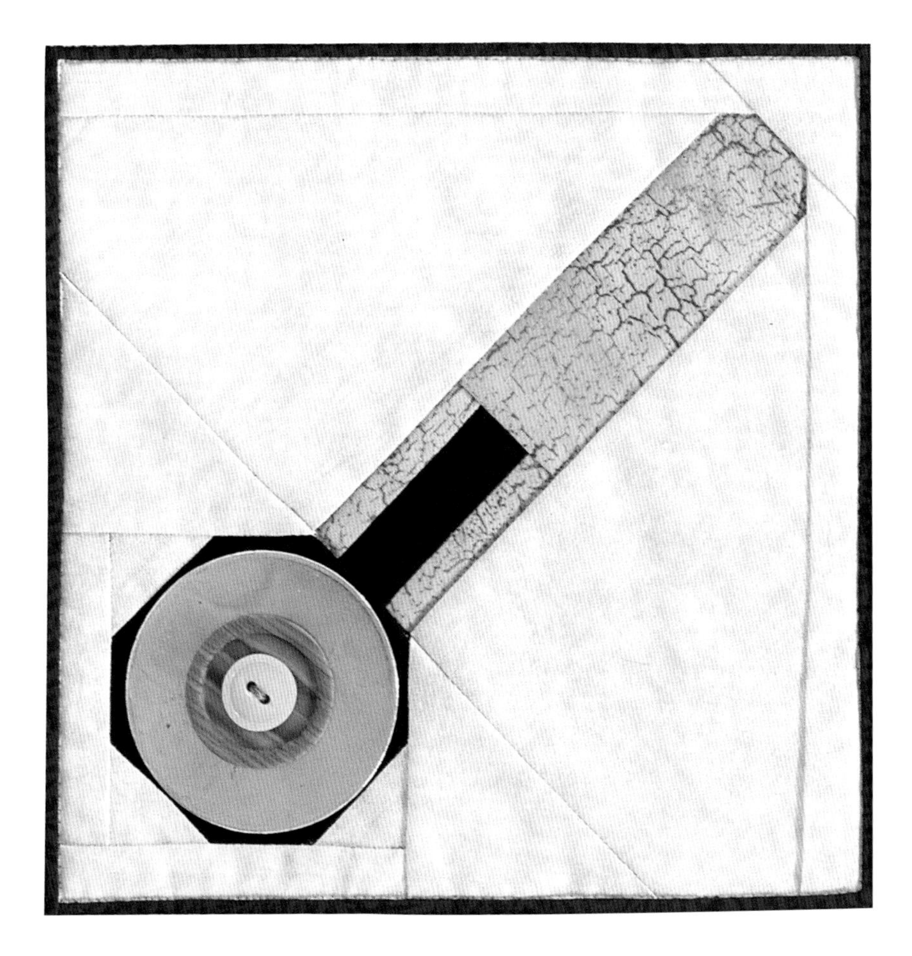

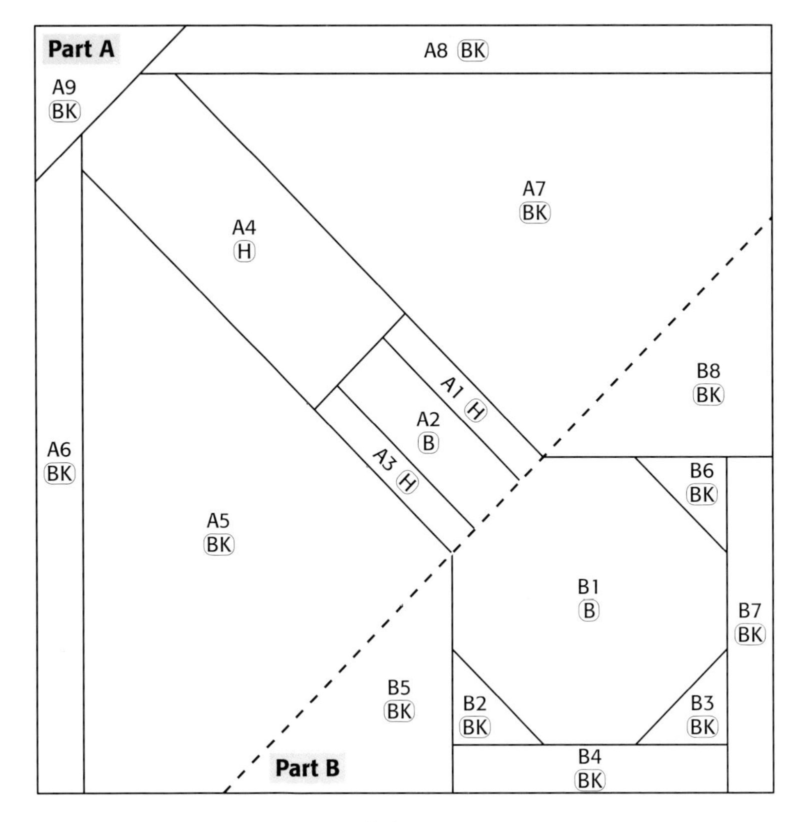

Foundation Pattern

SCISSORS

SNIP, SNIP. *Cut, cut. One pair is never enough! Paper scissors. Fabric scissors. Appliqué scissors. Embroidery scissors. Each one designed to perform a particular job better—and we want them all!*

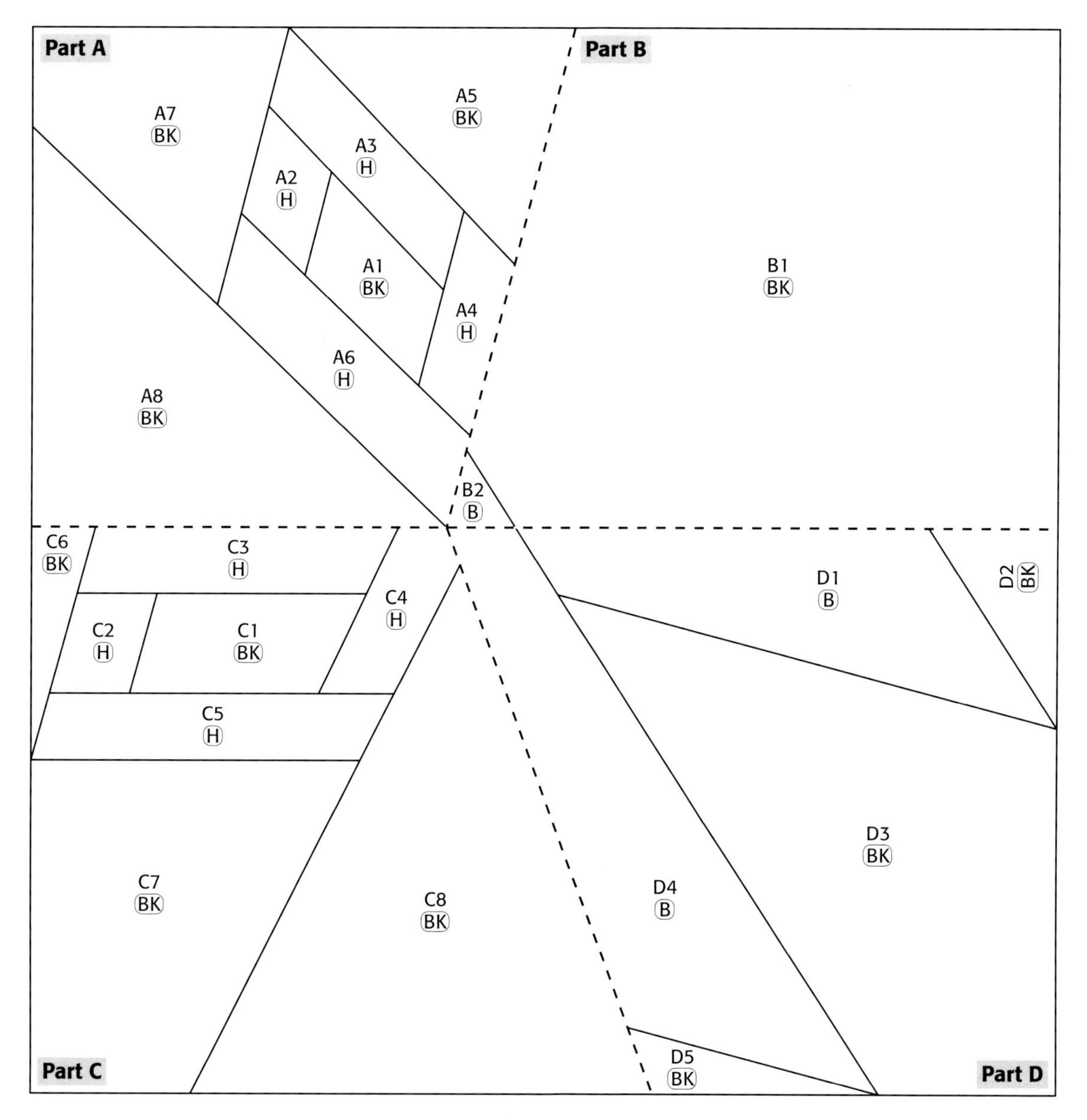

Foundation Pattern

Fabric Key

BK–Background

B–Blades

H–Handle

Sewing Order

Part A: 1–8

Part B: 1–2

Join A to B (AB)

Part C: 1–8

Part D: 1–5

Join C to D (CD)

Join AB to CD (ABCD)

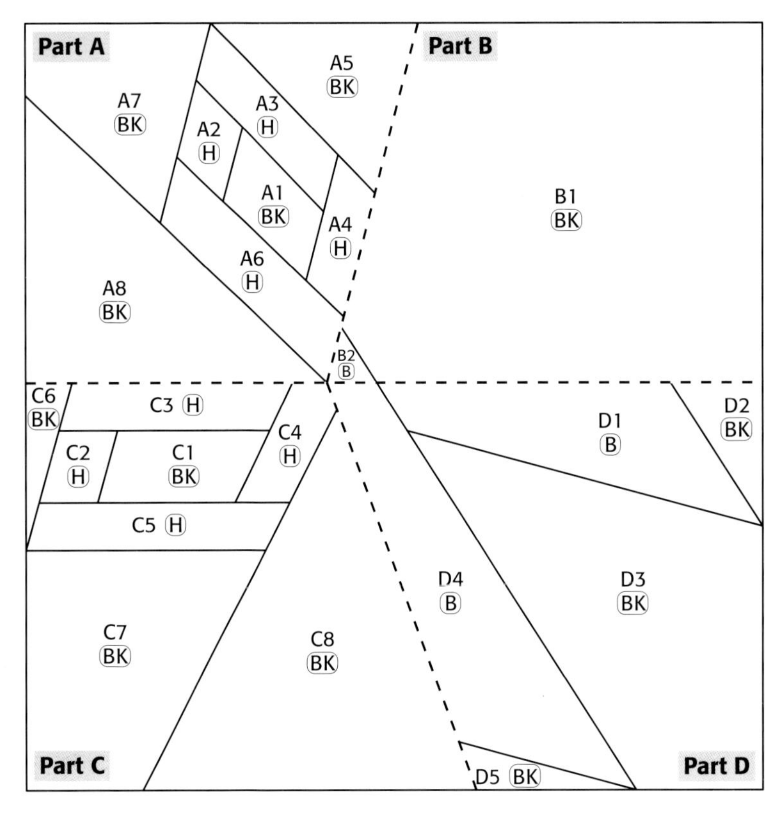

Foundation Pattern

SEAM RIPPER

On my class *lists, the seam ripper is generally listed as "optional—but probably necessary." Of course, as quilters, we all know that taking out stitches builds character. But just how much character does any one quilter really need?*

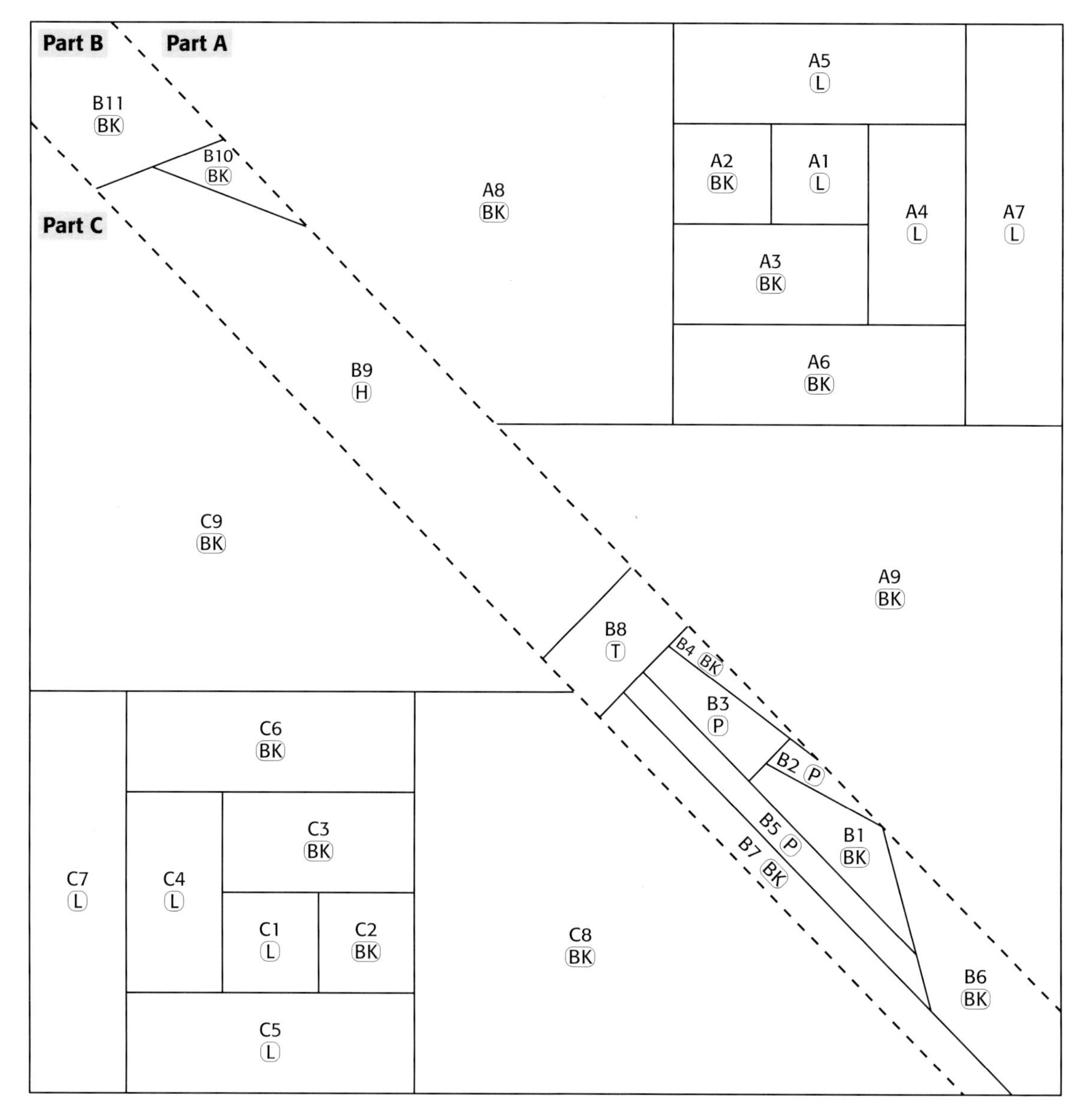

Foundation Pattern

Fabric Key

BK–Background

H–Handle

L–Log Cabin Corners

P–Point

T–Trim

Sewing Order

Part A: 1–9

Part B: 1–11

Join A to B (AB)

Part C: 1–9

Join AB to C (ABC)

Block Embellishment Guide

See page 55.

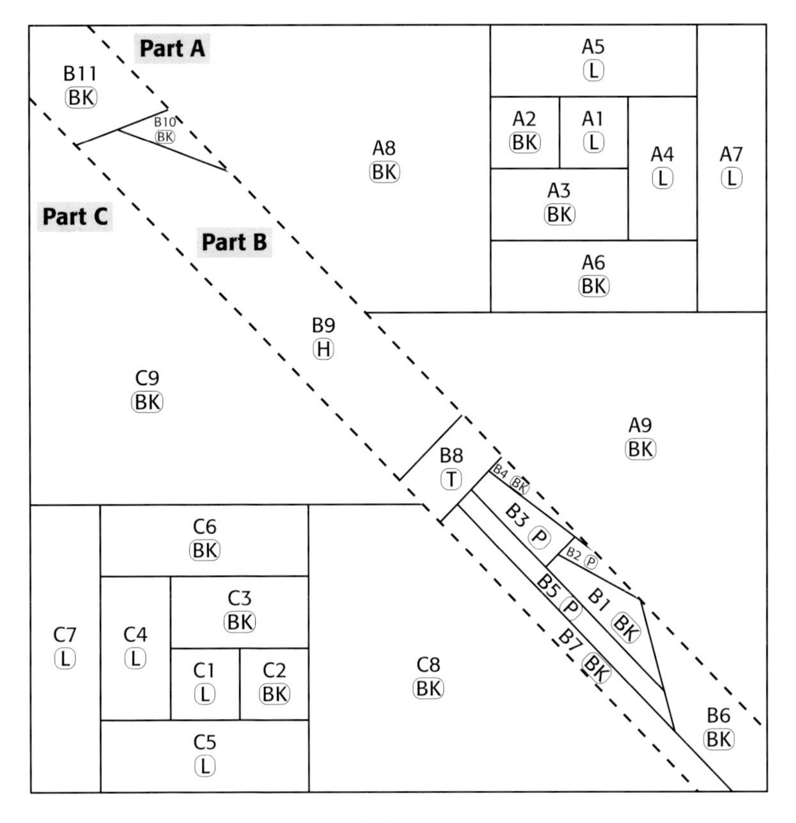

Foundation Pattern

SEWING MACHINE

BE IT AN *old Singer Featherweight or a brand new high-tech computer model, our sewing machine can easily become our best friend. We give it lots of time and attention, and our only wish is that it would come with an unending bobbin thread!*

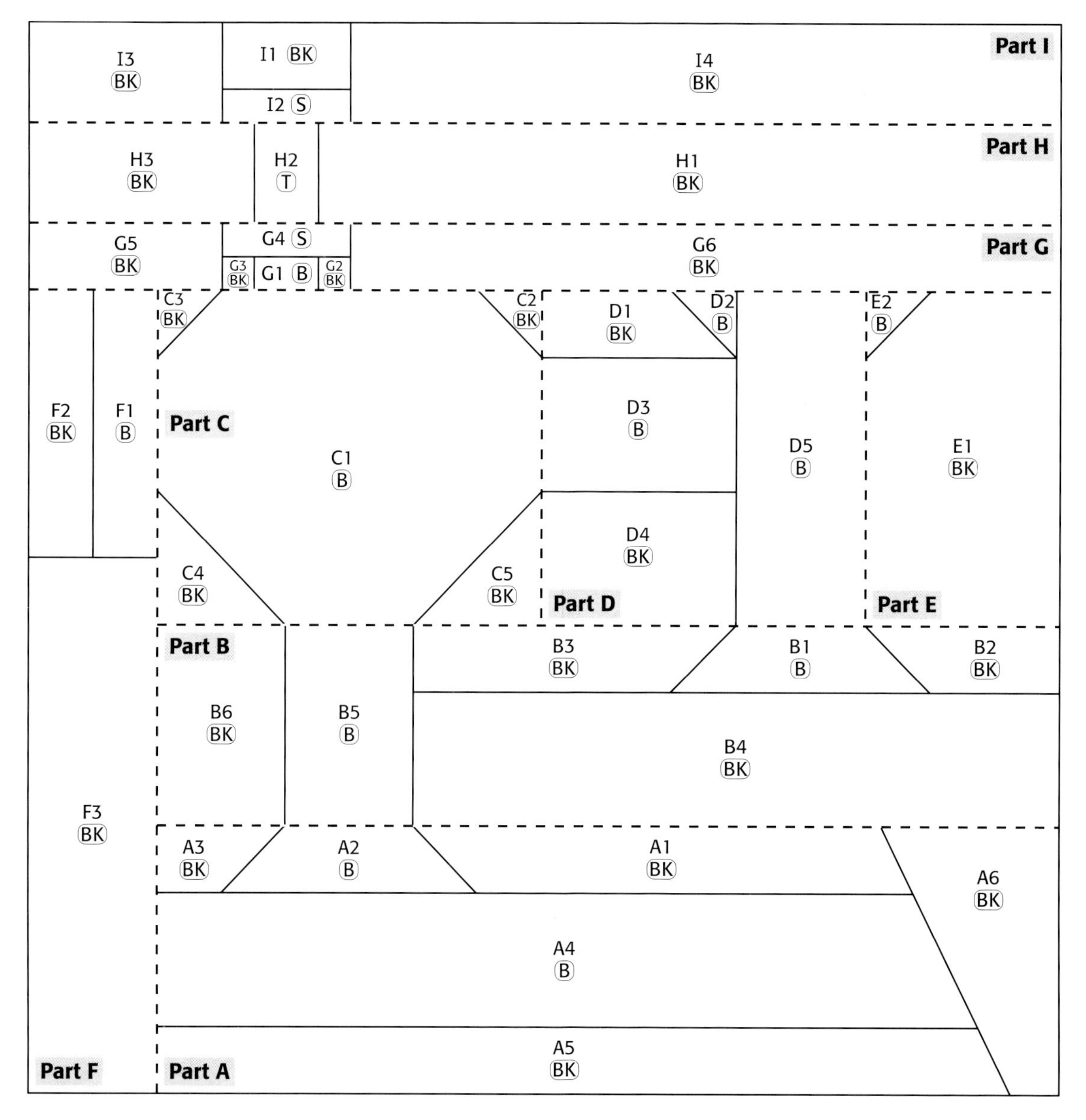

Foundation Pattern

Fabric Key

BK–Background
B–Body
S–Spool
T–Thread Color

Sewing Order

Part A: 1–6
Part B: 1–6
Join A to B (AB)
Part C: 1–5
Part D: 1–5
Join C to D (CD)
Part E: 1–2
Join CD to E (CDE)
Join AB to CDE (ABCDE)
Part F: 1–3
Join ABCDE to F (ABCDEF)
Part G: 1–6
Part H: 1–3
Join G to H (GH)
Part I: 1–4
Join GH to I (GHI)
Join ABCDEF to GHI
(ABCDEFGHI)

Block Embellishment Guide

See page 57.

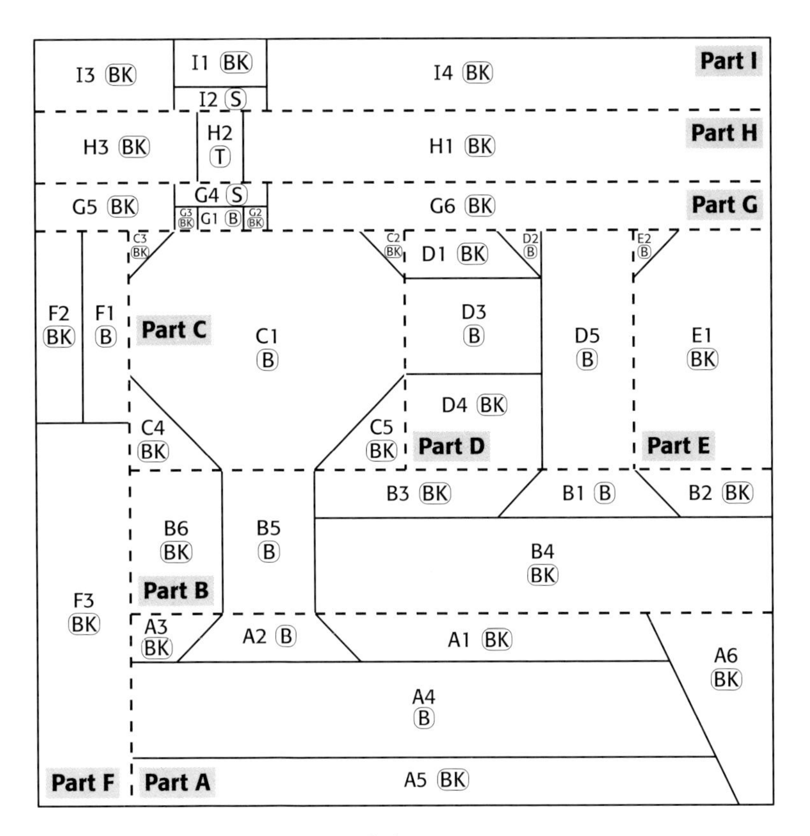

Foundation Pattern

SPOOLS OF THREAD

OUR SPOOLS OF *thread are our palettes of color and glory. Unfortunately, we never seem to have enough spools or colors to satisfy our insatiable appetite for these colorful notions.*

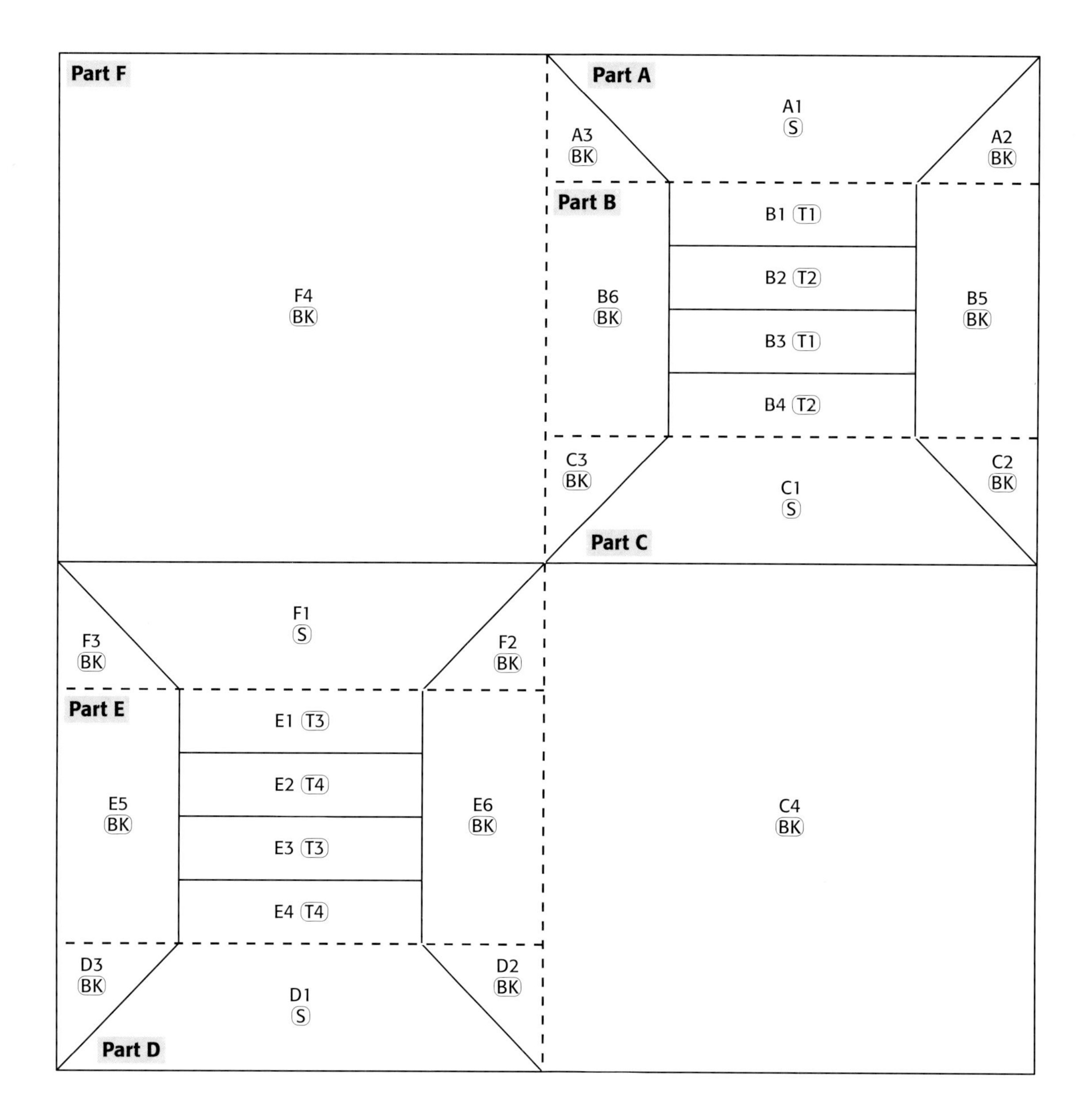

Fabric Key

BK–Background

S–Spool

T1–Thread 1 (Dark Color 1)

T2–Thread 2 (Medium Color 1)

T3–Thread 3 (Dark Color 2)

T4–Thread 4 (Medium Color 2)

Sewing Order

Part A: 1–3

Part B: 1–6

Join A to B (AB)

Part C: 1–4

Join AB to C (ABC)

Part D: 1–3

Part E: 1–6

Join D to E (DE)

Part F: 1–4

Join DE to F (DEF)

Join ABC to DEF (ABCDEF)

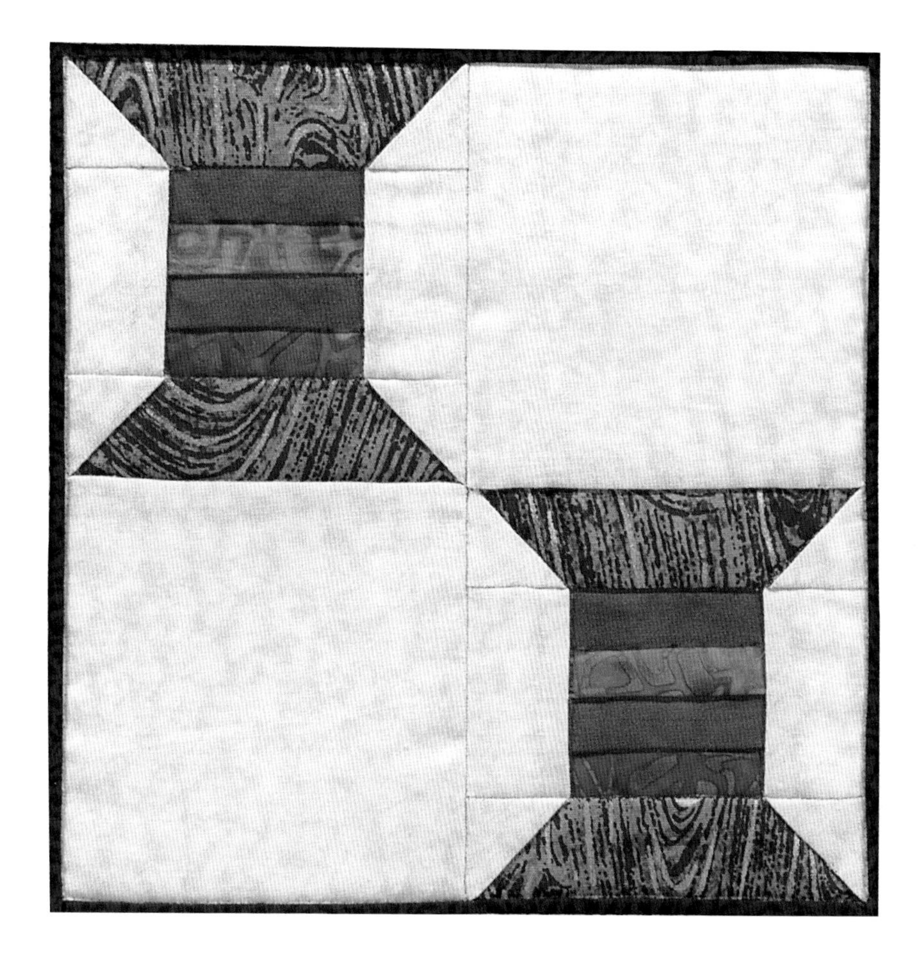

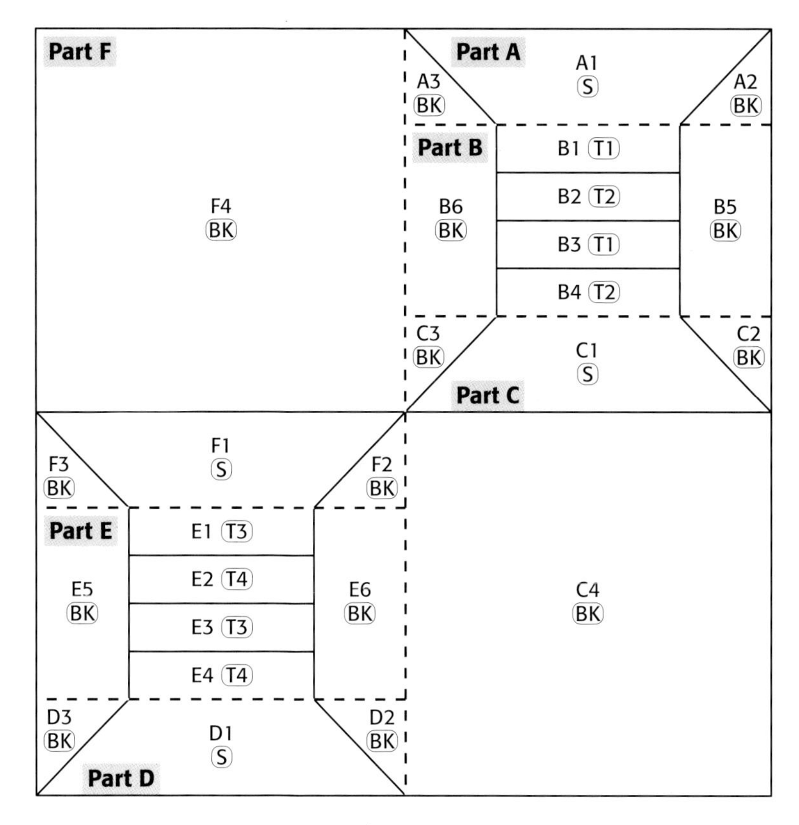

Foundation Pattern

TAPE MEASURE

"MEASURE TWICE. *Cut once." For some quilters perhaps it ought to be measure three or four times! In good quilting, workmanship and precision do count, and they begin with those first preliminary measurements.*

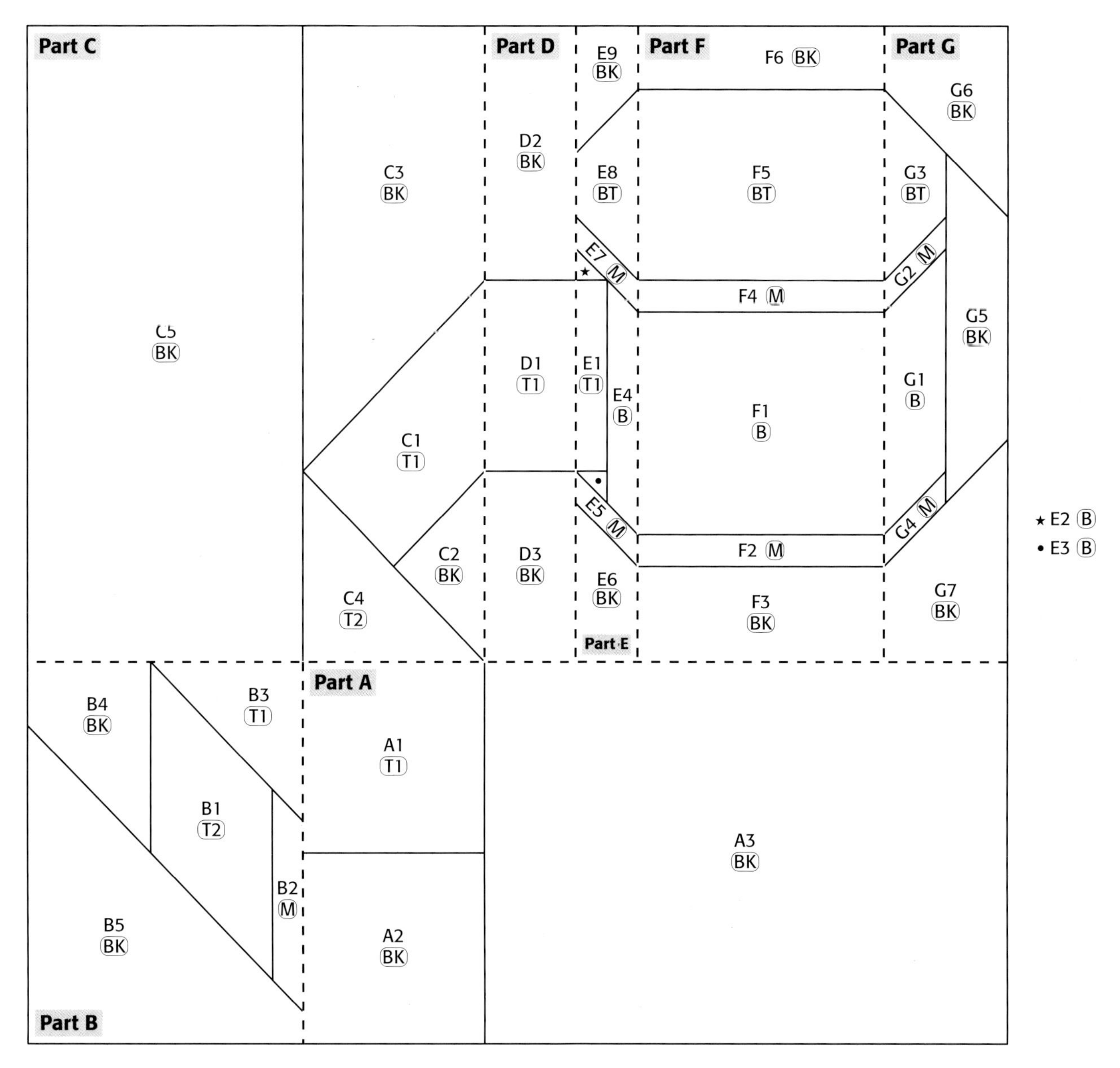

Foundation Pattern

Fabric Key

BK–Background

B–Box

BT–Box Top

M–Mitered Trim

T1–Tape 1

T2–Tape 2

Sewing Order

Part A: 1–3

Part B: 1–5

Join A to B (AB)

Part C: 1–5

Part D: 1–3

Join C to D (CD)

Part E: 1–9

Join CD to E (CDE)

Part F: 1–6

Join CDE to F (CDEF)

Part G: 1–7

Join CDEF to G (CDEFG)

Join AB to CDEFG (ABCDEFG)

Block Embellishment Guide

See page 56.

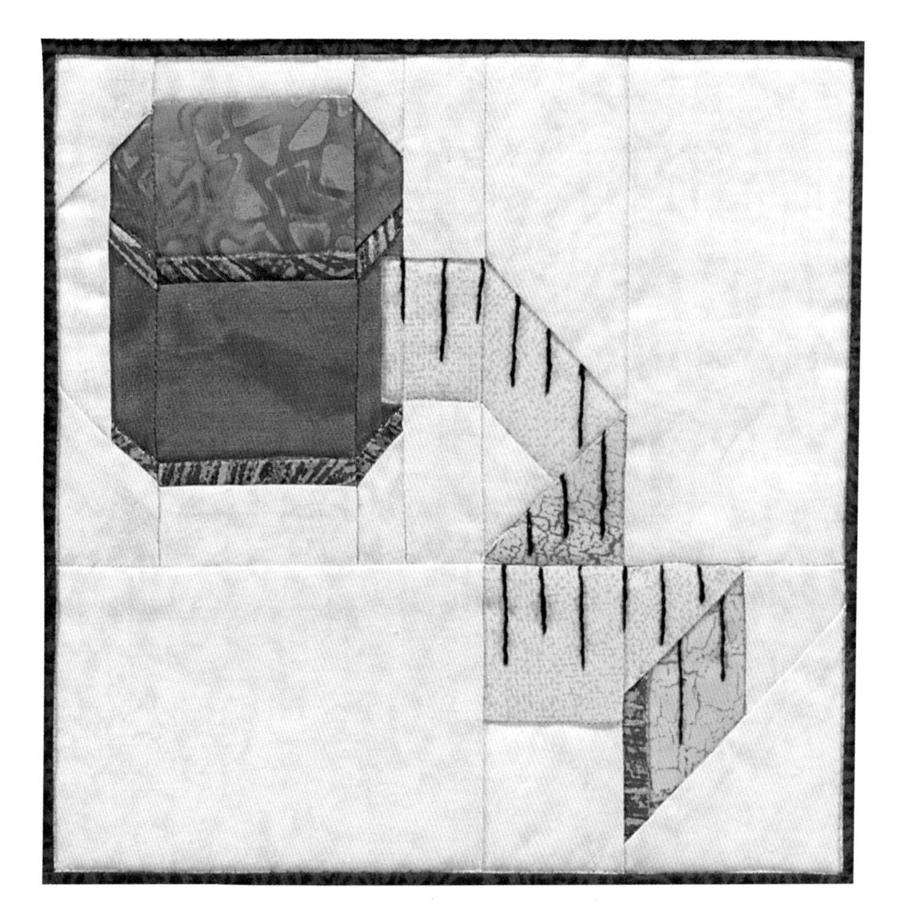

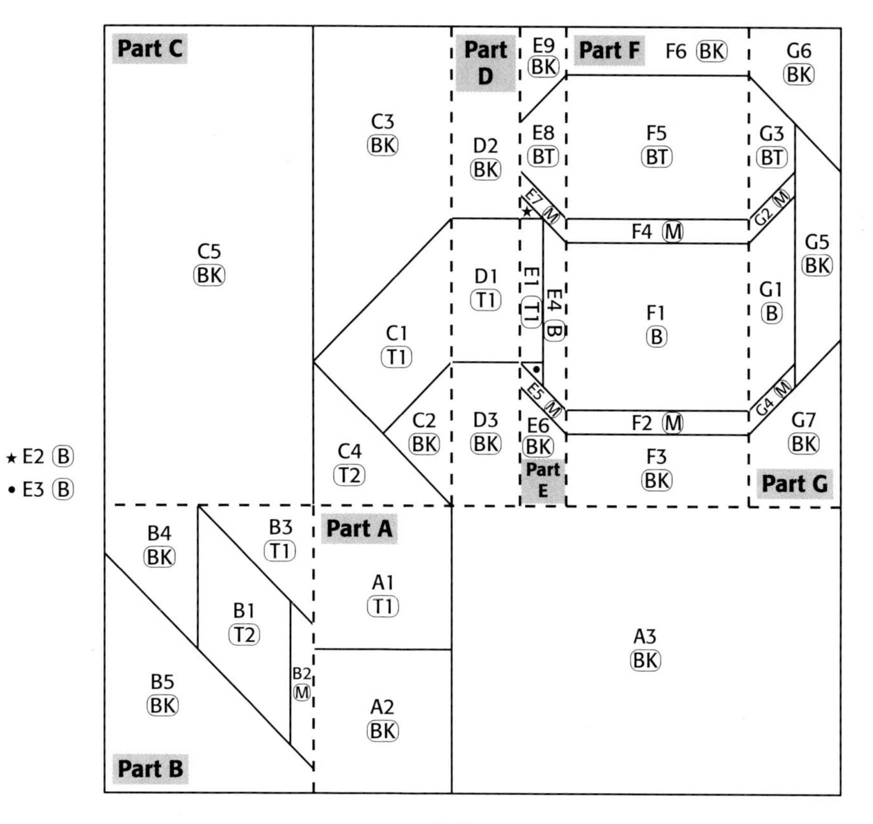

Foundation Pattern

THIMBLE

FINDING THE PERFECT *thimble is like the search for the Holy Grail. There ought to be a thimble motto: If you find one you like, buy two. It's a very personal thing.*

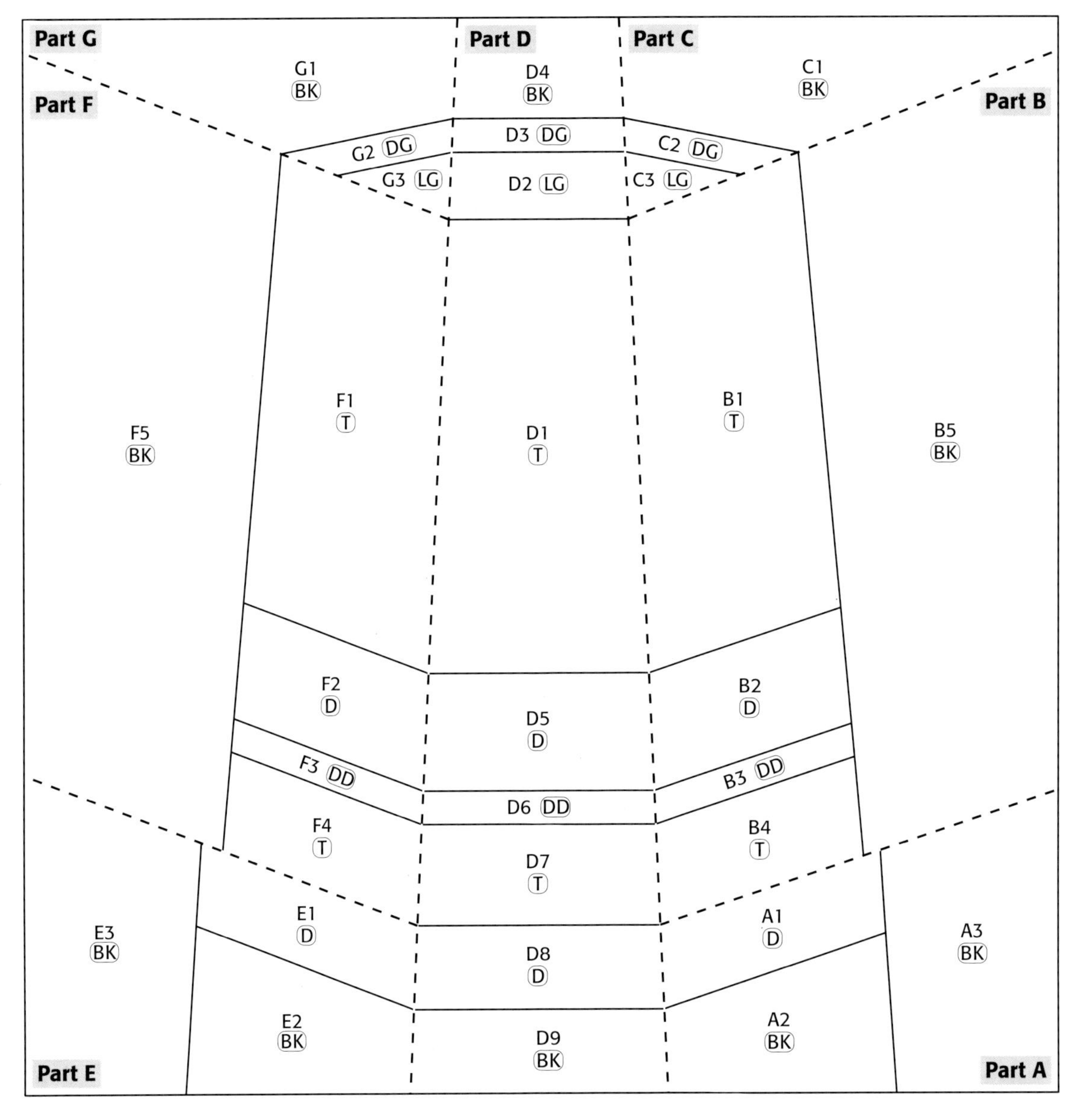

Foundation Pattern

Fabric Key

BK–Background

D–Decorative Edge

DD–Dark Decorative Edge

DG–Dark Gray

LG–Light Gray

T–Thimble

Sewing Order

Part A: 1–3

Part B: 1–5

Join A to B (AB)

Part C: 1–3

Join AB to C (ABC)

Part D: 1–9

Join ABC to D (ABCD)

Part E: 1–3

Part F: 1–5

Join E to F (EF)

Part G: 1–3

Join EF to G (EFG)

Join ABCD to EFG (ABCDEFG)

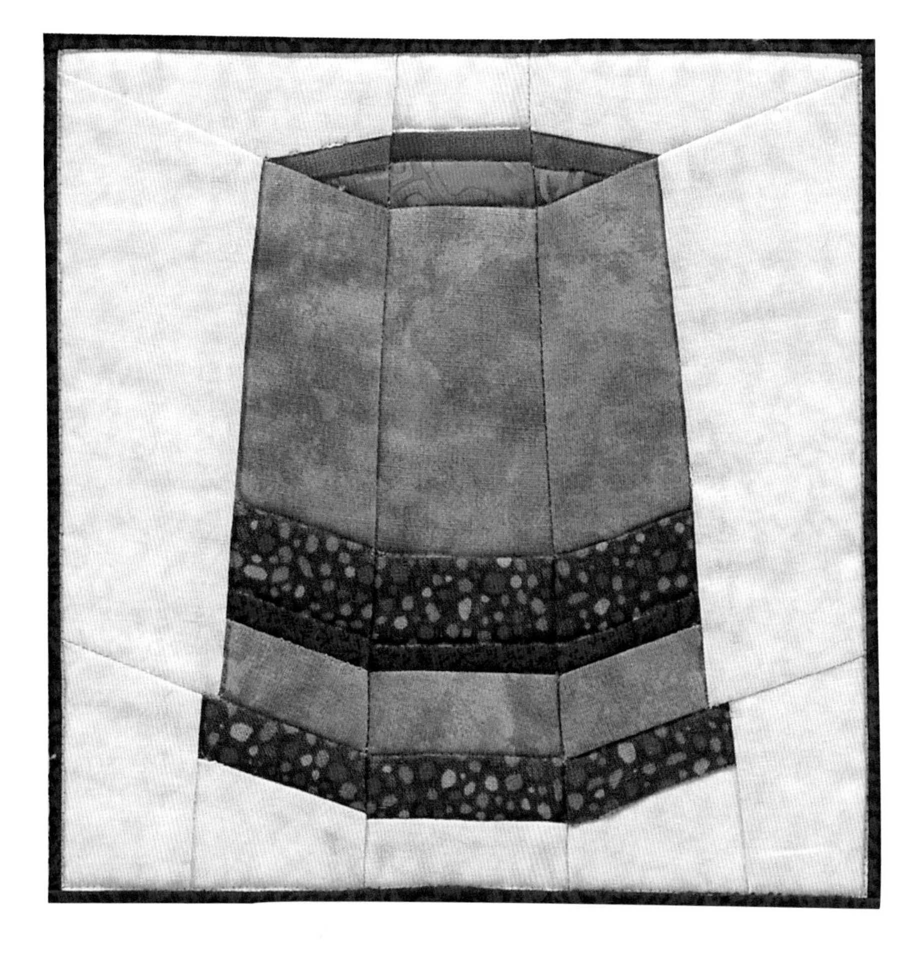

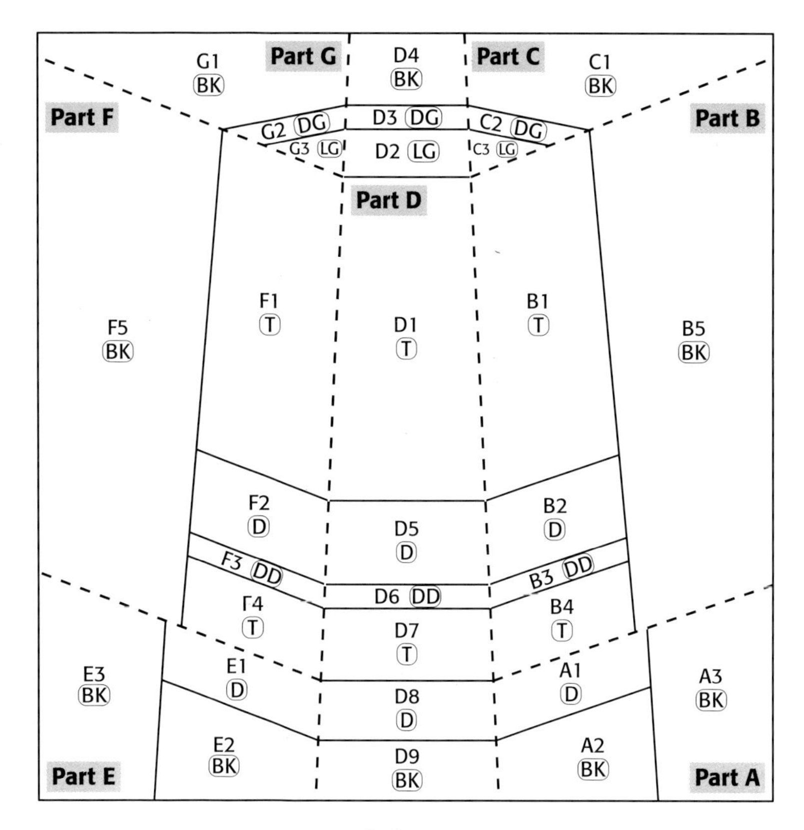

Foundation Pattern

SEWING ROOM SUE–DREAMING AND QUILTING

Finished Size: 10" x 14"

Fabric Key

BK–Background
B–Bonnet
C–Chair
D1–Dress 1
D2–Dress 2
F–Flesh
P–Quilt Patches (use a variety of fabrics)
T–Trim

Sewing Order

Part A: 1–9
Part B: 1–9
Join A to B (AB)
Part C: 1–10
Join AB to C (ABC)
Part D: 1–9
Join ABC to D (ABCD)
Part E: 1–5
Join ABCD to E (ABCDE)
Part F: 1–6
Part G: 1–6
Join F to G (FG)
Part H: 1–4
Part I: 1–3
Join H to I (HI)
Join ABCDE to HI (ABCDEHI)
Join ABCDEHI to FG (ABCDEFGHI)
Part J: 1–3
Part K: 1–4
Part L: 1–5
Join K to L (KL)
Part M: 1–5
Join KL to M (KLM)
Join J to KLM (JKLM)
Join ABCDEFGHI to JKLM (ABCDEFGHIJKLM)

CALLING ALL FANS *of Sunbonnet Sue who enjoy foundation piecing. "Sewing Room Sue" has been designed for you. Here she sits so comfortably in her rocking chair with her work-in-progress quilt spread across her lap.*

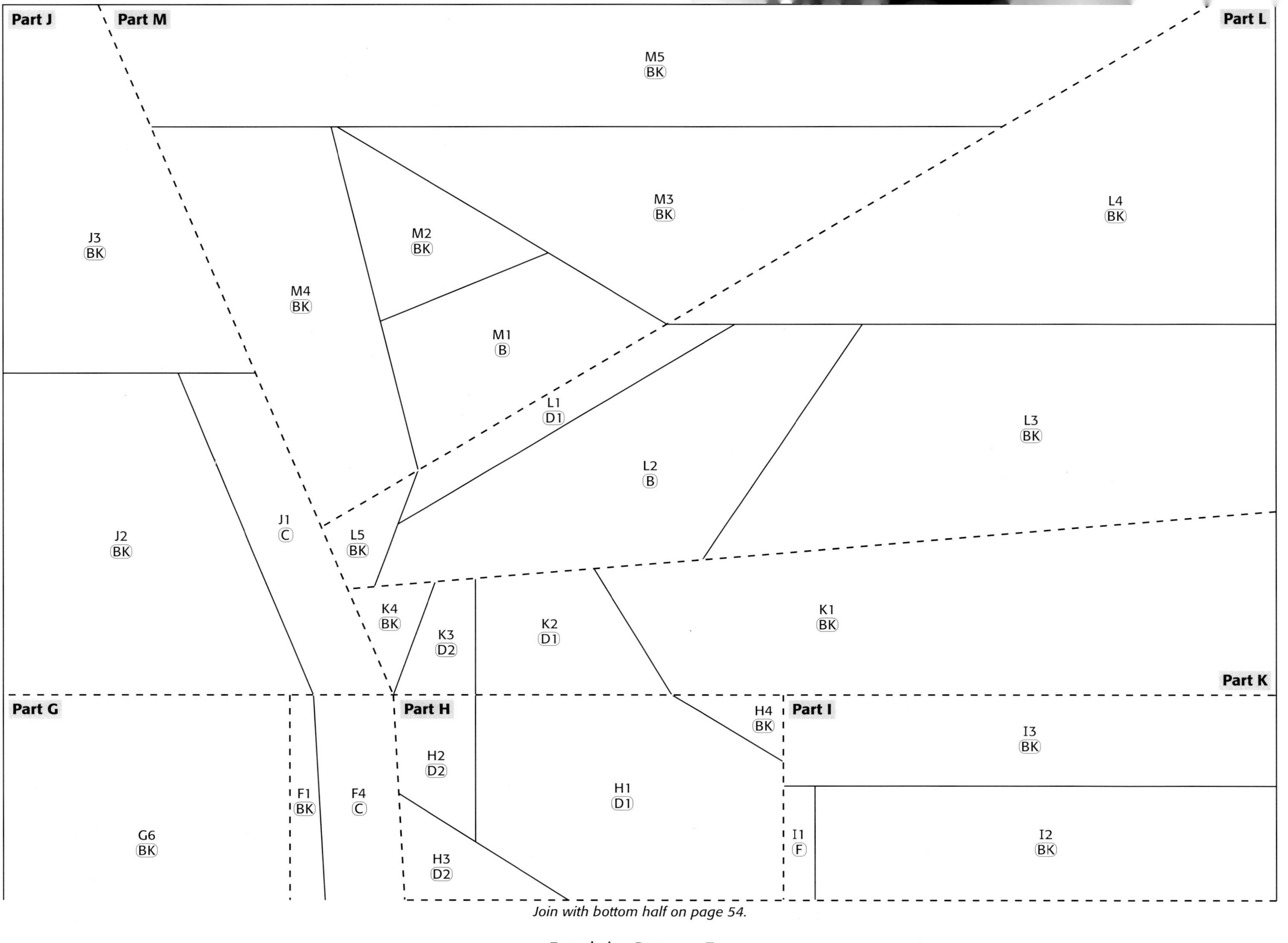

Join with bottom half on page 54.

Foundation Pattern – Top

Join with top half on page 53.

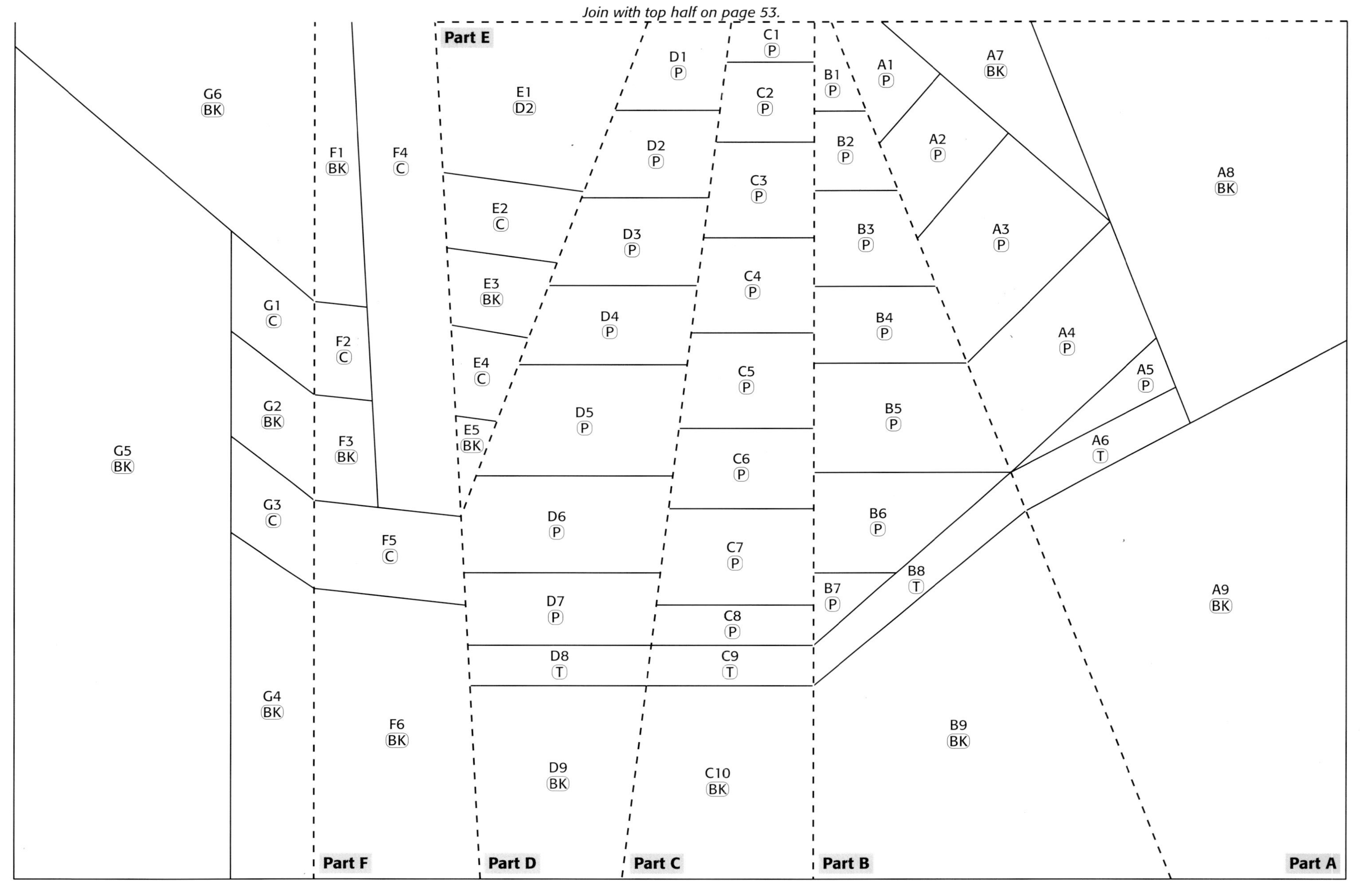

Foundation Pattern – Bottom

Block Embellishment Guides

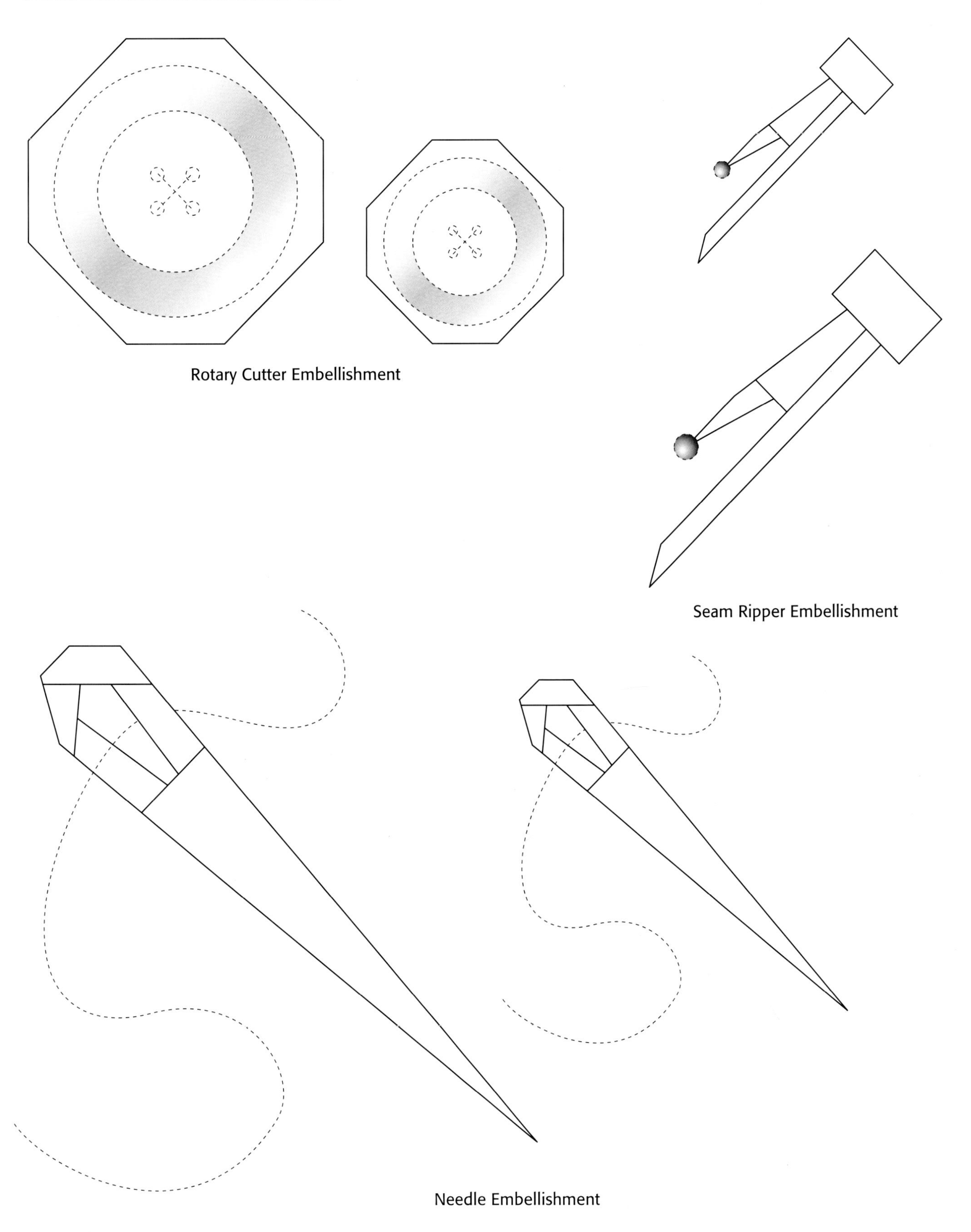

Rotary Cutter Embellishment

Seam Ripper Embellishment

Needle Embellishment

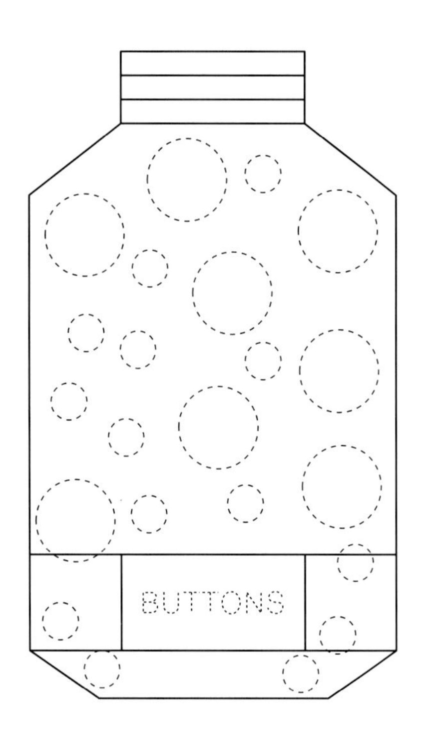

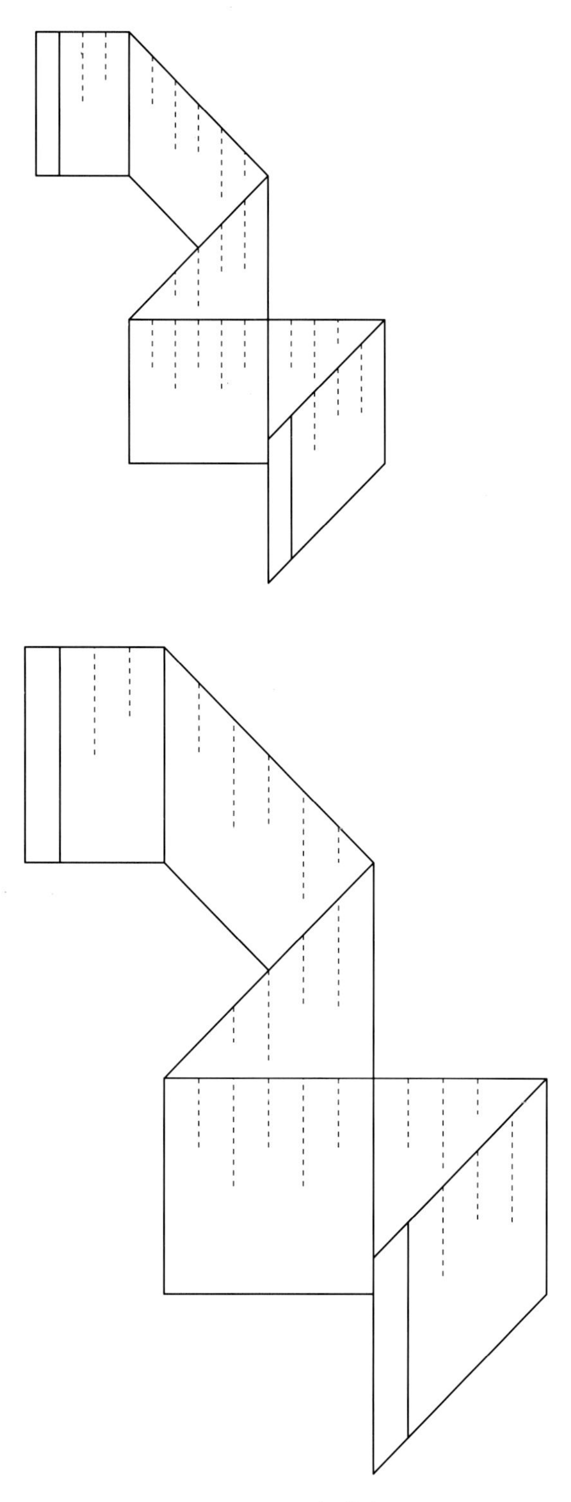

Tape Measure Embellishment

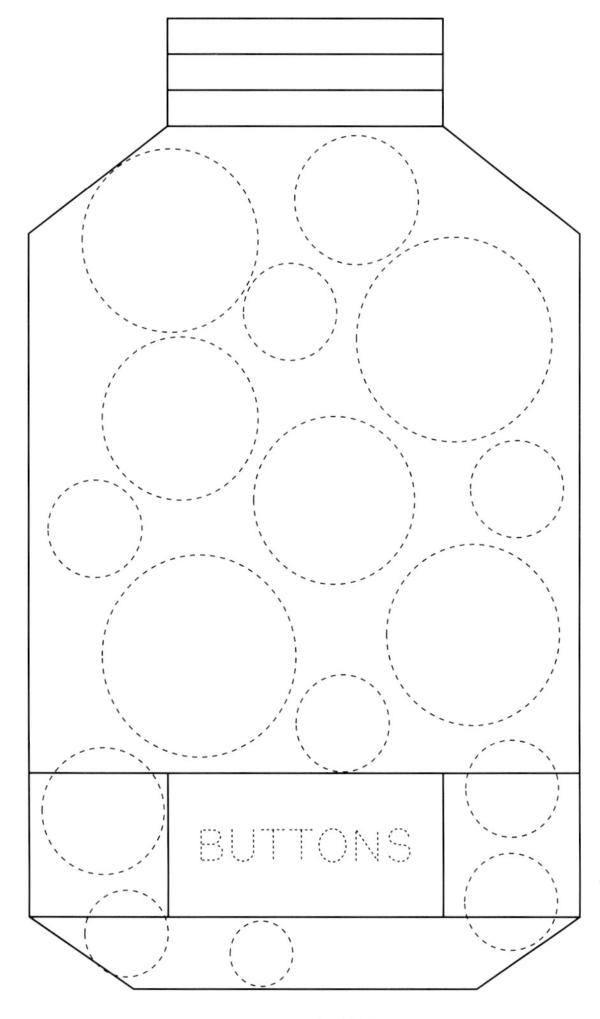

Button Jar Embellishment

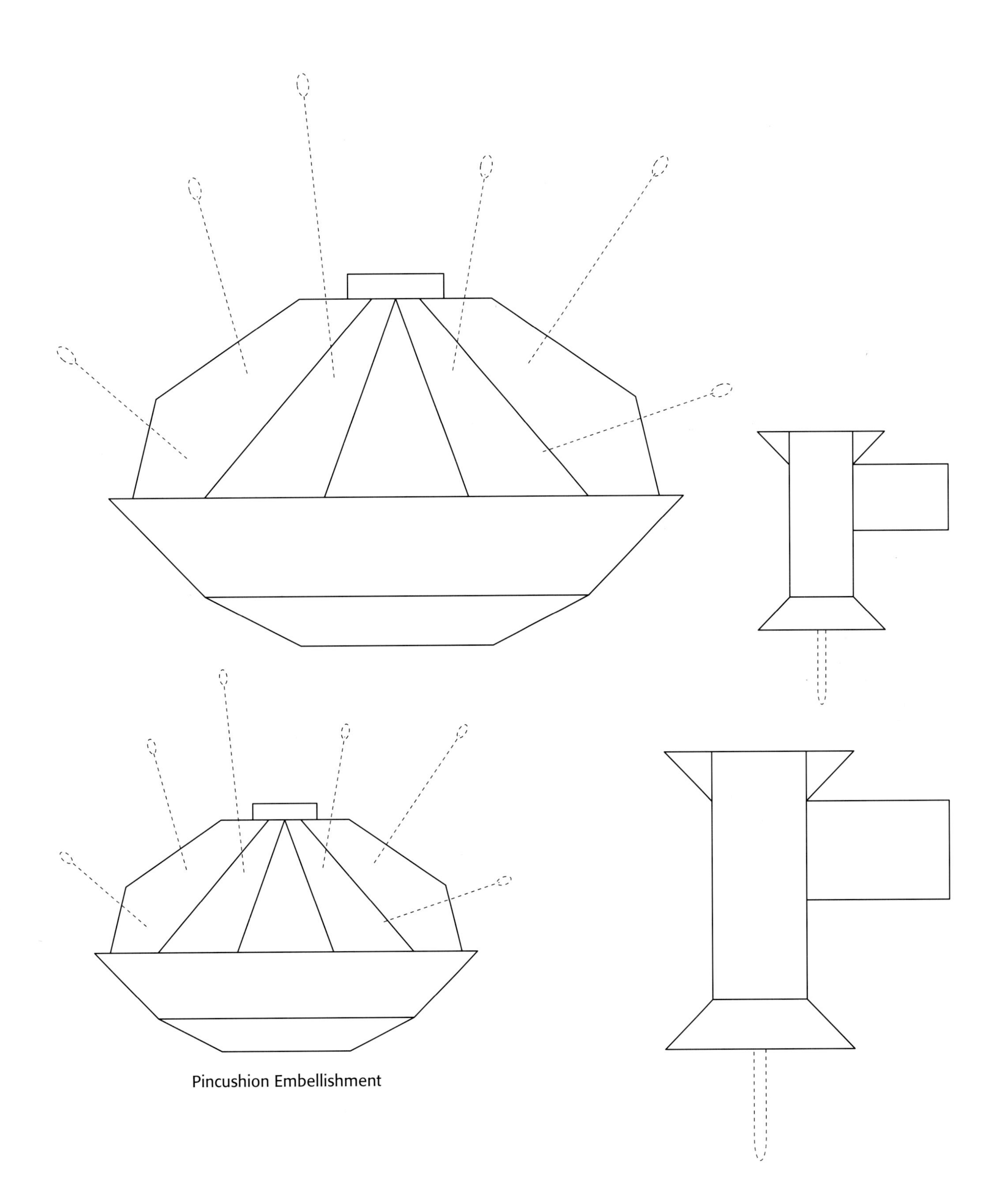

Pincushion Embellishment

Sewing Machine Embellishment

THE QUILTS

NEEDLES AND NOTIONS

THESE WALL HANGINGS *are an ideal size for smaller wall spaces, as a gift for a sewing friend, or for the small quilts needed for a guild silent auction. What sewer or quilter wouldn't enjoy a sewing machine wall quilt? And even a non-quilter would appreciate a cup-and-saucer wall hanging to grace her breakfast area. Choose to do only one, or do several and arrange them in a pleasing grouping. They are designed to look like framed pictures, so there is great flexibility in their placement. Enjoy creating your own attractive arrangement.*

Finished Size: 12" x 12"

Materials: *42"-wide fabric*

- 1/8 yd. or scrap for block background
- Assorted scraps for tool (refer to individual pattern for specific fabric number and type)
- 1/8 yd. or scrap for accent borders
- 1/8 yd. or scrap for inner border
- 3/8 yd. for outer border and binding
- 1 fat quarter (18" x 22") for backing and rod pocket
- 16" x 16" square of batting

Cutting

1. From the accent border fabric, cut:
   - 2 strips, each 3/4" x 42"; crosscut the strips to make the following pieces:
     - 2 strips, each 3/4" x 7", for inner accent border sides
     - 2 strips, each 3/4" x 7½", for inner accent border top and bottom
     - 2 strips, each 3/4" x 8½", for outer accent border sides
     - 2 strips, each 3/4" x 9", for outer accent border top and bottom
2. From the inner border fabric, cut:
   - 1 strip, 1¼" x 42"; crosscut the strip to make the following pieces:
     - 2 strips, each 1¼" x 7", for inner border sides
     - 2 strips, each 1¼" x 8¾", for inner border top and bottom
3. From the outer border and binding fabric, cut:
   - 2 strips, each 2½" x 42", for outer border; crosscut the strips to make the following pieces:
     - 2 strips, each 2½" x 9", for outer border sides
     - 2 strips, each 2½" x 13", for outer border top and bottom
   - 2 strips, each 2" x 42", for binding
4. From the backing fabric, cut:
   - 1 square, 16" x 16", for backing
   - 1 piece, 4" x 12", for rod pocket

Quilt Top Assembly

1. Trace the 6" freezer-paper foundation pattern for the desired tool onto freezer paper.
2. Refer to "Step by Step to Successful Paper Foundation Piecing" (pages 11–17) to construct the block, following the Sewing Order and Fabric Key for the desired block (pages 28–51). Each block should measure 6½" x 6½" before adding any borders. If it does not, be sure to adjust the border-strip cut lengths accordingly.
3. Refer to "Accenting the Positive" (pages 17–19) for directions on applying the inner accent border, then the inner border. Repeat to apply the outer accent border and outer border.

Quilt Finishing

Refer to "Finishing Touches" on pages 20–26.

1. Embroider any block details.
2. Layer the quilt top with batting and backing; baste.
3. Quilt as desired.
4. Square up the quilt top.
5. Add the rod pocket and bind the quilt.
6. Add any desired bead or button embellishments.
7. Stitch a label to the quilt back.

Quilt in the ditch around each part of the sewing notion and then along each separate border. In the outer border, add two additional rows of channel quilting approximately ½" from the seam line and the binding edge.

Sewing Room Sue—Dreaming and Quilting

WOULDN'T WE ALL *like to have the time to sit quietly, stitching and daydreaming of quilts yet begun! Sunbonnet Sue sits so comfortably in her rocking chair with her work-in-progress quilt spread across her lap.*

Finished Size: 17" x 21"

Materials: *42"-wide fabric*

- ¼ yd. for background fabric
- 4" x 22" or larger piece for rocking chair
- Assorted scraps for Sue's dress, blouse, bonnet, bonnet trim, and flesh
- 5 to 7 coordinating scraps, plus scraps of the outer and accent border fabrics, for the lap quilt
- ⅛ yd. for accent borders
- ⅛ yd. or scrap for inner border
- ½ yd. for outer border and binding
- 24" x 28" piece for backing
- 24" x 28" piece of batting

Cutting

After cutting the following pieces, use the remaining fabrics in the block.

1. From the accent border fabric, cut:
   - 3 strips, each ¾" x 42"; crosscut the strips to make the following pieces:
     - 2 strips, each ¾" x 13", for inner side accent border
     - 2 strips, each ¾" x 9", for inner top and bottom accent border
     - 2 strips, each ¾" x 15", for outer side accent border
     - 2 strips, each ¾" x 11½", for outer top and bottom accent border
2. From the inner border fabric, cut:
   - 2 strips, each 1⅜" x 42"; crosscut the strips to make the following pieces:
     - 2 strips, each 1⅜" x 13", for inner side borders
     - 2 strips, each 1⅜" x 11", for top and bottom borders
3. From the outer border and binding fabric, cut :
   - 2 strips, each 4" x 42"; crosscut the strips to make the following pieces:
     - 2 strips, each 4" x 15", for outer side borders
     - 2 strips, each 4" x 18½", for outer top and bottom borders
   - 2 strips, each 2" x 42", for binding

Quilt Top Assembly

1. Using the foundation pattern for Sewing Room Sue—Dreaming and Quilting, trace 1 pattern.
2. Refer to "Step by Step to Foundation Piecing" (pages 11-17) to construct the block, following the Sewing Order and Fabric Key (page 52). Using your rotary cutting equipment, trim "Sue" to 8½" x 12¼".

Note: *Sue's original block size was deliberately designed to be larger than necessary so she could be trimmed to fit into a variety of settings.*

3. Refer to "Accenting the Positive" (pages 17-19) to apply the inner accent border, then the inner border. Repeat to apply the outer accent border and outer border.

Quilt Finishing

Refer to "Finishing Touches" on pages 20–26.

1. Embroider any block details.
2. Layer the quilt top with batting and backing; baste.
3. Quilt as desired.
4. Square up the quilt top.
5. Add the rod pocket and bind the quilt.
6. Add any desired bead or button embellishments.
7. Stitch a label to the quilt back.

Quilt in the ditch around the units of Sue's dress, blouse, bonnet, bonnet trim, hands, chair, and around every single patch on her quilt. Stipple quilt the background, then quilt in the ditch of the borders, adding rows of channel quilting in the outer border.

SEWING ROOM SAMPLER:

ROW BY ROW, NOTION BY NOTION

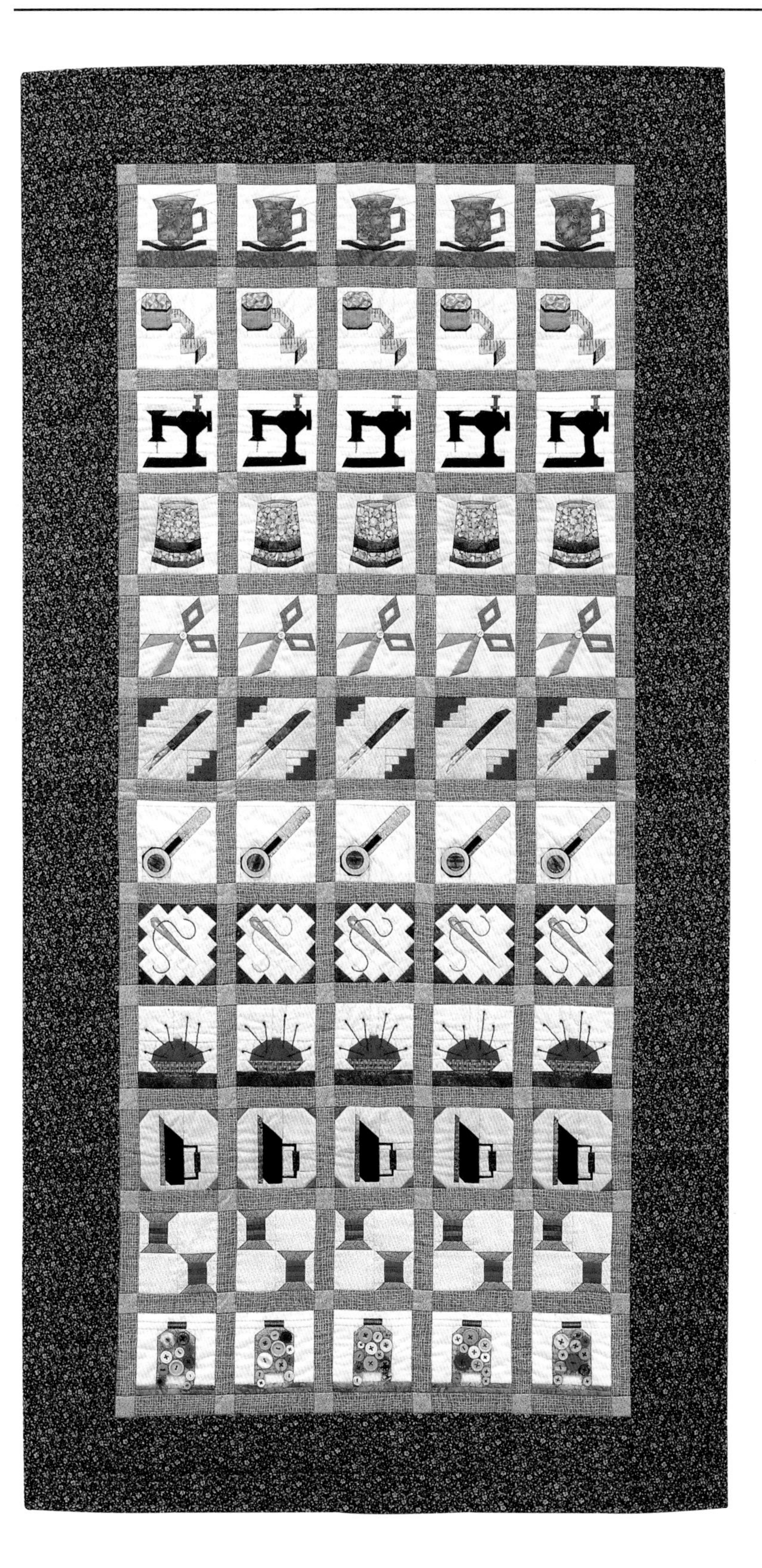

THE TWELVE BLOCK *designs used in this quilt were originally presented as a block-of-the-month program at my quilt shop, Idle-Hour Quilts and Design, in 1998. Every month each participant received one of the 4" paper foundation patterns with a fabric kit large enough to complete five blocks of the design. The goal was to sew one horizontal row every month and eventually build a quilt, row by row. The quilt featured here is the result.*

FINISHED SIZE: 35" x 70"

MATERIALS: *42"-wide fabric*

- Assorted fabrics and embellishments for 60 Needles and Notions blocks (refer to "Row Fabric Requirements" on page 64 for suggested fabric amounts for 1 row)
- ¾ yd. for sashing
- ¼ yd. for corner posts
- 2⅛ yds. for outer border and binding
- 2⅜ yds. for backing and rod pocket
- 42" x 76" piece of batting

Row Fabric Requirements

The following fabric amounts will complete one row of the same notion.

Button Jar

1/4 yd.	Bk–Background
6" x 22"	J–Jar
6" x 10"	L1–Lid 1
6" x 6"	L2–Lid 2
3" x 5"	N–Neutral for Label
6" x 22"	T–Table

Cup and Saucer

1/4 yd.	BK–Background
1/8 yd.	C–Cup
6" x 6"	I–Inside of Cup
6" x 22"	S–Saucer
6" x 11"	T–Tabletop

Iron

1/4 yd.	BK–Background
6" x 22"	B–Body
6" x 9"	C–Corners
6" x 6"	H–Handle
6" x 9"	P–Plate

Needle

1/4 yd.	BK–Background
10" x 11"	B–Border
4" x 22"	N–Needle

Pincushion

1/4 yd.	BK–Background
4" x 22"	B–Basket
9" x 11"	P1–Pincushion 1
9" x 6"	P2–Pincushion 2
5" x 22"	T–Table

Rotary Cutter

1/4 yd.	BK–Background
9" x 11"	B–Blade
9" x 11"	H–Handle

Scissors

1/4 yd.	BK–Background
6" x 22"	B–Blade
7" x 22"	H–Handle

Seam Ripper

1/4 yd.	BK–Background
8" x 6"	H–Handle
1/8 yd.	L–Log Cabin Corners
8" x 6"	P–Point
6" x 6"	T–Trim

Sewing Machine

1/4 yd.	BK–Background
1/8 yd.	B–Body
6" x 6"	S–Spool
Scraps	T–Thread (use 5 different colors)

Spools of Thread

1/8 yd.	BK–Background
9" x 11"	S–Spools
5" x 11"	T1–Thread 1
5" x 11"	T2–Thread 2
5" x 11"	T3–Thread 3
5" x 11"	T4–Thread 4

Tape Measure

1/4 yd.	BK–Background
9" x 9"	B–Box
6" x 9"	BT–Box Top
6" x 9"	M–Mitered Trim
9" x 11"	T1–Tape 1
9" x 9"	T2–Tape 2

Thimble

1/4 yd.	BK–Background
6" x 9"	D–Decorative Edge
6" x 9"	DD–Dark Decorative Edge
6" x 9"	DG–Dark Gray
6" x 9"	LG–Light Gray
6" x 22"	T–Thimble

Cutting

1. From the sashing fabric, cut 18 strips, each 1½" x 42"; crosscut the strips to make 137 strips, each 1½" x 4½".
2. From the corner post fabric, cut 3 strips, each 1½" x 42"; crosscut the strips to make 78 squares, each 1½" x 1½".
3. From the outer border fabric, cut:
   - 3 strips, each 5" x 76", for side, top, and bottom outer borders
   - 3 strips, each 2" x 76", for binding

Quilt Top Assembly

1. Using the 4" foundation patterns for the 12 Needles and Notions blocks on pages 28–51, trace 5 of each pattern for a total of 60 blocks.
2. Refer to "Step by Step to Successful Paper Foundation Piecing" (pages 11–17), to construct the blocks, following the Sewing Order and Fabric Key for each individual block (pages 28–51).
3. Arrange the rows in the desired order.
4. To make the sashing rows, sew together 6 corner posts and 5 sashing strips, beginning and ending with a corner post. Make 13. Press the seams toward the sashing strips.

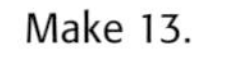

Make 13.

5. To make the block rows, stitch together 6 sashing strips and 5 blocks of the same notion, beginning and ending with a sashing strip. Make 12. Press the seams toward the sashing strips.

Make 12.

6. Alternating sashing and block rows, stitch rows together, beginning and ending with a sashing row.
7. Measure the quilt top through the center to determine the length. Cut 2 outer border side strips to the exact measurement. Stitch the strips to the quilt sides.
8. Measure the quilt top through the center, including the borders, to determine the width. Using the remaining outer border strip, cut the top and bottom border strips to the exact measurement and stitch to the quilt top and bottom edges.

Quilt Finishing

Refer to "Finishing Touches" on pages 20–26.

1. Embroider the block details.
2. Layer the quilt top with batting and backing; baste.
3. Quilt as desired.
4. Square up the quilt top.
5. Add a rod pocket and bind the quilt.
6. Add any desired bead or button embellishments.
7. Stitch a label to the quilt back.

Quilt in the ditch around all the notions parts and in all the seams of the sashing, corner posts, and borders. In addition, add more lines of channel quilting to the outer border.

TUTTI-FRUTTI

Do you have *an impossibly tall, narrow area within your home that needs to be filled? Is your foyer replete with high ceilings and bare walls? Or do you have a stairwell area that could accommodate a narrow, full-length wall hanging? "Tutti-Frutti" can fill the bill.*

Finished Size: 19" x 94"

Materials: *42"-wide fabric*

- 1½ yds. for block background
- ⅜ yd. for accent border and blocks
- ⅛ yd. each of 8 to 10 assorted fabrics for blocks and pieced inner border
- ⅞ yd. for middle border and sashing
- 3 yds. for outer border and binding
- 2¼ yds. for backing and rod pocket

Cutting

After cutting the following pieces, use the remaining fabrics in the blocks.

1. From the accent border fabric, cut 8 strips, each ¾" x 42".
2. From each of the 8 to 10 assorted fabrics, cut 1 strip, 1½" x 42", for the pieced inner border.
3. From the middle border and sashing fabric, cut:
   - 6 strips, each 1⅜" x 42", for middle border
   - 3 strips, each 1⅜" x 42", for horizontal sashing
   - 5 strips, each 1⅜" x 42", for vertical sashing
4. From the outer border and binding fabric, cut:
   - 3 strips, each 2" x 99", for binding
   - 1 strip, 4" x 99", for top and bottom borders
   - 2 strips, each 4" x 99", for side borders

Quilt Top Assembly

1. Using the 6" freezer-paper foundation patterns for the Needles and Notions blocks on pages 28–51, trace 1 each of the 12 patterns.

2. Refer to "Step by Step to Successful Paper Foundation Piecing" (pages 11–17) to construct the blocks, following the Sewing Order and Fabric Key for each individual block (pages 28–51).

3. Refer to "Accenting the Positive" (pages 17–19) to apply the accent border strips to each block. Measure each block; each one should be approximately the same size when finished.

4. Arrange the blocks vertically as desired.

5. From the horizontal sashing strips, crosscut 13 segments the block length. Alternately stitch the sashing strips and blocks together, beginning and ending with a sashing strip (see illustration at right).

6. Cut 1 vertical sashing strip in half widthwise. Piece 2 full lengths and 1 half length together, end to end. Repeat for the remaining vertical sashing strips. Stitch the strips to the quilt sides. Trim the strips even with the top and bottom.

7. To assemble the pieced inner border, stitch the 1½" x 42" assorted fabric strips together along the long edges. Press the seam allowances to 1 side.

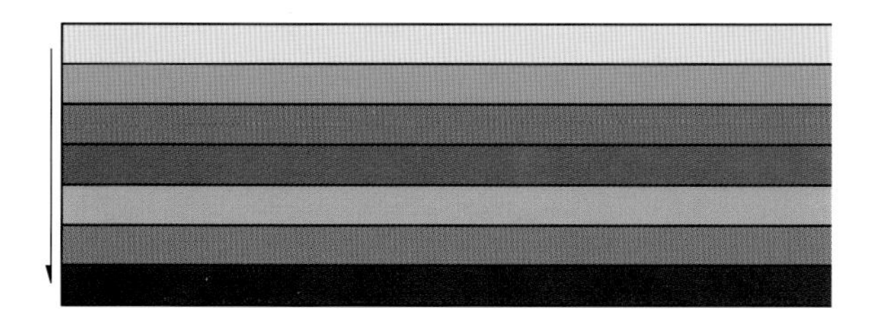

8. Using your rotary-cutting equipment, crosscut the pieced unit into 1½"-wide segments. Depending on the number of fabrics used, you will need approximately 25 to 27 segments. Stitch the segments together, end to end. You will need approximately 87 squares for each side border and 8 each for the top and bottom borders.

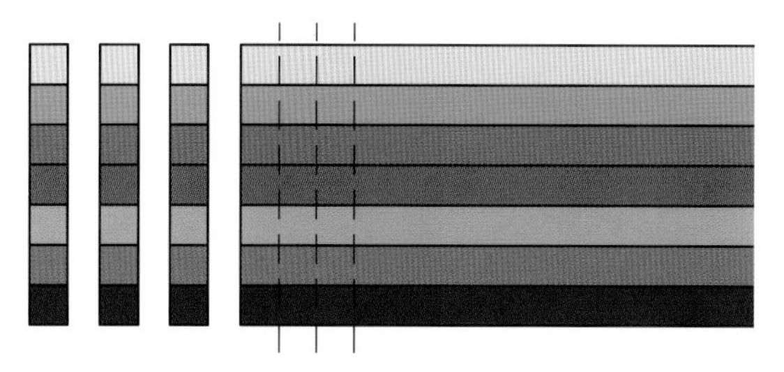

9. Stitch the pieced border to the quilt in the following order: top, side, bottom, side. Be sure to follow the color order established earlier. Some adjustments may be needed to avoid having the same color blocks next to each other.

10. Stitch 3 middle border strips together, end to end. Repeat for the remaining 3 middle border strips. Measure the quilt width and cut the exact length from each of the 2 pieced strips. Stitch the strips to the quilt top and bottom. Stitch the remaining lengths to the quilt sides.

11. Cut the top/bottom outer border strip in half widthwise and stitch to the quilt top and bottom. Trim the ends even with the sides. Stitch the side border strips to each side; trim the ends even with the top and bottom.

Quilt Finishing

Refer to "Finishing Touches" on pages 20–26.

1. Embroider the block details.
2. Layer the quilt top with batting and backing; baste.
3. Quilt as desired.
4. Square up the quilt top.
5. Add a rod pocket and bind the quilt.
6. Add any desired bead or button embellishments.
7. Stitch a label to the quilt back.

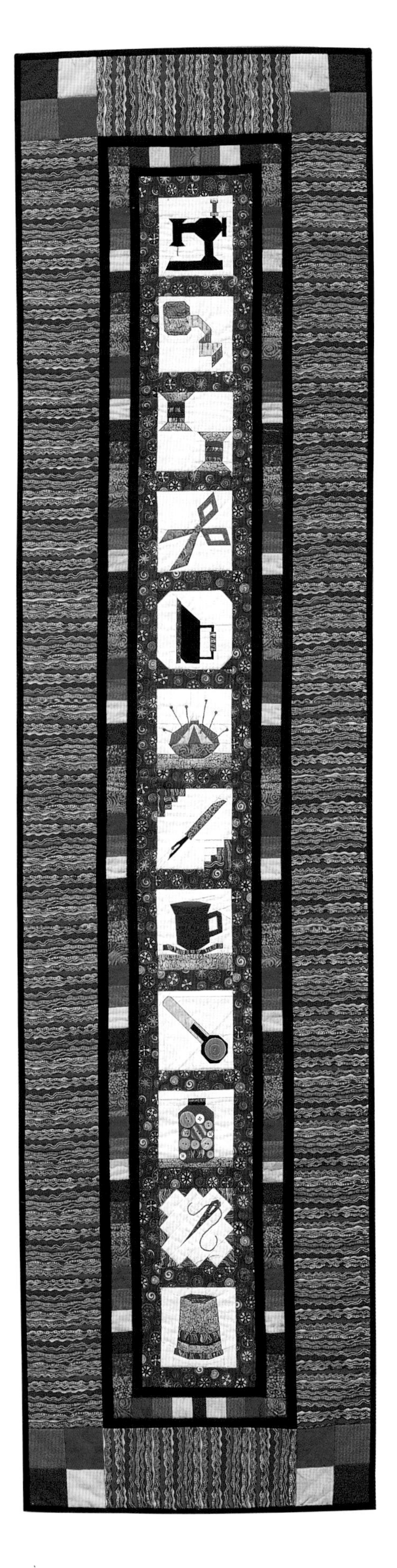

CALYPSO—FLIP 'N' SEW!

WOW! POP! BOOM! *Sizzle! Let your spirits soar, and choose some wild and wonderful fabrics that shout color and joy! Pull out all those bright, bright intense colors and use them to make the Needles and Notions blocks sing! Carry the color excitement out to the multiple borders, and suddenly your quilt top is a happening thing!*

FINISHED SIZE: 18" x 73"

MATERIALS: *42"-wide fabric*

- 1 yd. for block background
- 1/8 yd. each or scraps of 8 to 10 assorted fabrics for blocks and pieced border
- 3/8 yd. for sashing
- 3/4 yd. for inner borders and binding
- 2 yds. for outer border
- 2 yds. for backing and rod pocket
- 22" x 77" piece of batting

CUTTING

After cutting the following pieces, use the remaining fabrics in the blocks.

1. From each of the 8 to 10 assorted fabrics, cut 1 strip, 1½" x 42", for the pieced border.
2. From the sashing fabric, cut 6 strips, each 1½" x 42"; crosscut 2 of the strips into 13 strips, each 1½" x 4½".
3. From the inner border and binding fabric, cut:
   - 10 strips, each 1" x 42", for narrow inner borders
   - 5 strips, each 2" x 42", for binding
4. From the outer border fabric, cut 3 strips, each 4½" x 76".

Quilt Top Assembly

1. Using the 4" foundation patterns for the Needles and Notions blocks on pages 28–51, trace 1 each of the 12 patterns.

2. Refer to "Step by Step to Successful Paper Foundation Piecing" (pages 11–17), to construct the blocks, following the Sewing Order and Fabric Key for each individual block (pages 28–51).

3. Arrange the 12 blocks vertically as desired. Alternately stitch the 1½" x 4½" sashing strips and blocks together, beginning and ending with a sashing strip (see illustration at right).

4. From the remaining sashing strips, join 2 lengths together, end to end; repeat for the remaining 2 lengths. Stitch the pieced sashing strips to the quilt sides. Trim the ends even with the top and bottom.

5. Measure the quilt through the center to determine the width. From 1 inner border strip, cut 2 strips to that exact measurement. Stitch the strips to the quilt top and bottom. Trim the ends even with the sides. Measure the quilt through the center, including the top and bottom borders, to determine the length. Stitch 2 remaining strips together, end to end, and cut to that exact measurement. Sew the strips to the quilt side. Repeat for the remaining side. Trim the ends even with the top and bottom. Set aside the trimmed pieces and remaining strips for the border that follows the pieced border.

6. To assemble the pieced border, stitch the 1½" x 42" assorted fabric strips together along the lengthwise edges. Press the seam allowances to 1 side.

7. Using your rotary-cutting equipment, crosscut the pieced unit into 1½"-wide segments. You will need approximately 20 to 22 segments for the border, depending on the number of fabrics used. Stitch the segments together, end to end. You will need approximately 62 squares for each side and 9 squares each for the top and bottom.

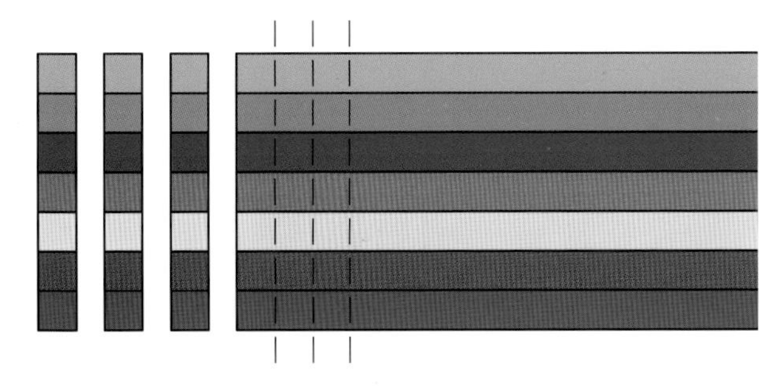

8. Stitch the pieced border to the quilt sides, being sure to space the blocks evenly and match the color order on each side. Measure the quilt width. Measure the top and bottom strip length. If the measurements differ, adjust the strip length by taking a wider seam allowance at the center block. Stitch the top and bottom strips to the quilt top and bottom edges.

9. Refer to step 5 to apply the next inner border, using the remaining inner border strips and trimmed pieces.

10. From 4 of the remaining pieced border fabrics, cut 4 squares from each fabric, each 2½" x 2½", for a total of 16 squares. Stitch 1 square of each color together as shown to create a Four Patch block.

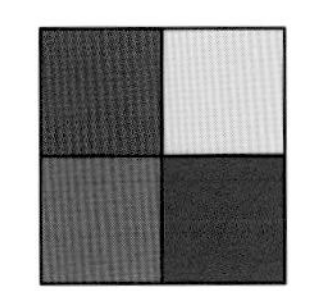

Upper left corner

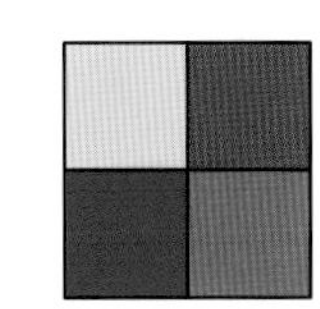

Upper right corner

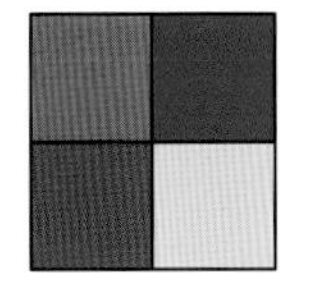

Lower left corner

Lower right corner

11. To make the outer pieced top and bottom border, measure the quilt width. From 1 outer border strip, cut 2 segments the measured width. Stitch a Four Patch block to each strip end; set aside.

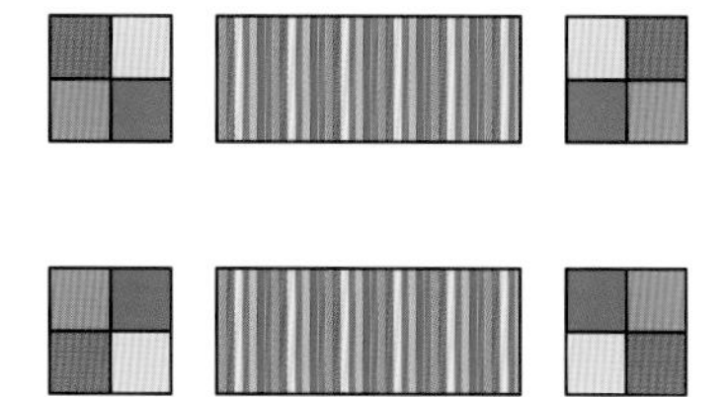

12. Stitch the remaining outer border strips to the quilt sides. Trim the ends even with the top and bottom. Stitch the pieced top and bottom borders to the quilt top and bottom edges.

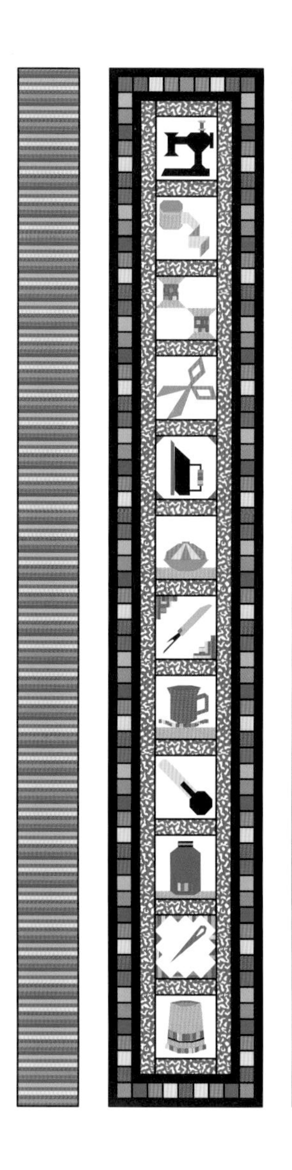

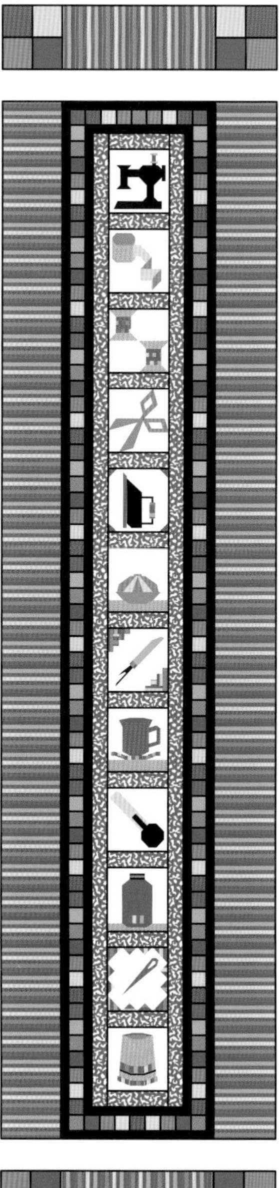

Quilt Finishing

Refer to "Finishing Touches" on pages 20–26.

1. Embroider the block details.
2. Layer the quilt top with batting and backing; baste.
3. Quilt as desired.
4. Square up the quilt top.
5. Add a rod pocket and bind the quilt.
6. Add any desired bead or button embellishments.
7. Stitch a label to the quilt back.

COUNTRY SAMPLER

DO YOU OR *your friends favor the warm hospitality that country decorating offers? If so, this quilt is for you. Select traditional country colors for the 6" blocks and sashing, then follow through on the country theme by choosing a homespun plaid for the outer border, a deep country blue for the inner border, and a barn red solid for the accent border and outer border corner squares. Add the final country touch by stitching a tiny white button to the corners of each corner post.*

Finished Size: 34" x 41"

Materials: *42"-wide fabric*

- 1½ yds. for block background
- ⅛ yd. each or scraps of 10 to 12 assorted fabrics for blocks
- ½ yd. for sashing
- ⅜ yd. for sashing corner posts and binding
- ¼ yd. for inner border
- ⅜ yd. for accent border and outer border corner posts
- ⅝ yd. for outer border
- 40" x 50" piece of backing fabric
- 40" x 50" piece of batting
- 80 buttons, ¼"-diameter

Cutting

After cutting the following pieces, use the remaining fabrics in the blocks.

1. From the sashing fabric, cut 6 strips, each 2" x 42"; crosscut the strips to make 31 strips, each 2" x 6½".
2. From the sashing corner post and binding fabric, cut:
   - 1 strip, 2" x 42"; crosscut into 20 squares, each 2" x 2" for sashing corner posts
   - 4 strips, each 2" x 42", for binding
3. From the inner border fabric, cut 4 strips, each 1½" x 42".
4. From the accent border and outer border corner post fabric, cut:
   - 4 strips, each ¾" x 42", for accent border
   - 4 blocks, each 4" x 4", for outer border corner posts
5. From the outer border fabric, cut:
   - 4 strips, each 4" x 42", for outer border

Quilt Top Assembly

1. Using the 6" paper patterns for the Needles and Notions blocks on pages 28–51, trace 1 each of the 12 patterns.
2. Refer to "Step by Step to Successful Paper Foundation Piecing" (pages 11–17) to construct the blocks, following the Sewing Order and Fabric Key for each individual block (pages 28–51).
3. Arrange the blocks in 4 rows of 3 blocks each.
4. To make the sashing rows, alternately sew together 4 corner posts and 3 sashing strips, beginning and ending with a corner post. Make 5. Press the seam allowances toward the sashing.

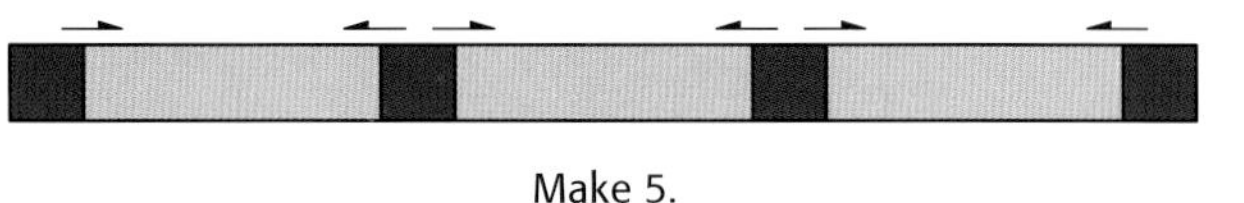

Make 5.

5. To make the block rows, alternately stitch together 4 sashing strips and 3 blocks, beginning and ending with a sashing strip. Make 4. Press the seam allowances toward the sashing.

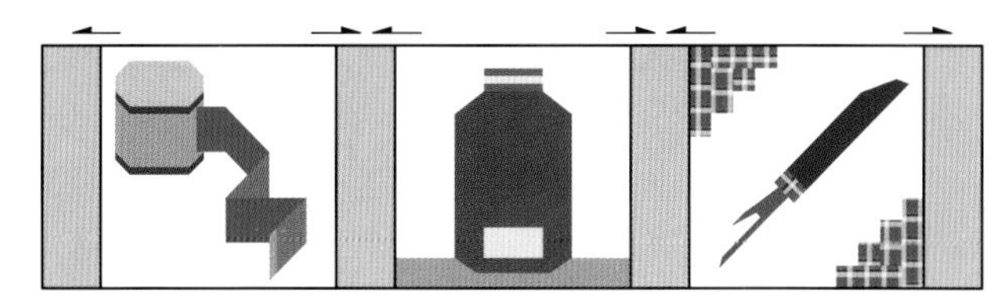

Make 4.

6. Alternating sashing and block rows, stitch rows together, beginning and ending with a sashing row.

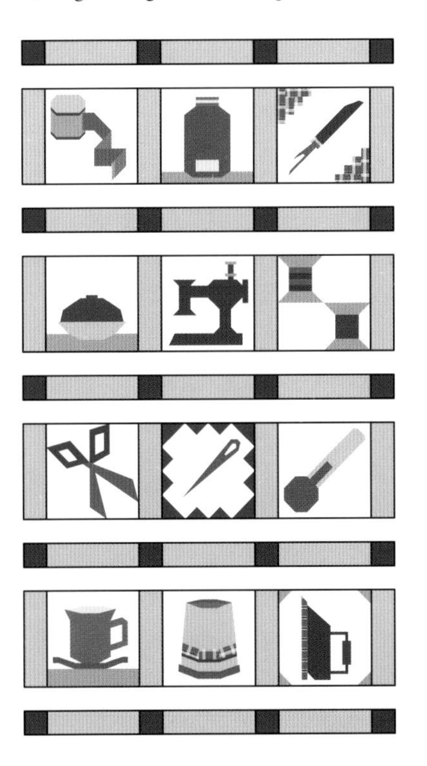

7. Measure the quilt top length. Cut 2 inner border strips to the exact measurement and stitch to the quilt sides.

8. Measure the quilt top width. Cut the remaining 2 inner border strips to the exact measurement and stitch the strips to the quilt top and bottom edge.

9. Refer to "Accenting the Positive" (pages 17–19) to add the accent border strips.

10. Measure the quilt top through the center to determine its length and width. Cut 2 outer border strips the quilt length measurement for the sides; cut 2 outer border strips the quilt width measurement for the top and bottom edges. Continue to refer to "Accenting the Positive" (pages 17–19) to stitch the side borders to the quilt sides. Trim the ends even with the top and bottom. Stitch the outer border corner posts to each end of the top and bottom strips. Stitch the pieced strips to the quilt top and bottom edges.

Quilt Finishing

Refer to "Finishing Touches" on pages 20–26.

1. Embroider the block details.
2. Layer the quilt top with batting and backing; baste.
3. Quilt as desired.
4. Square up the quilt top.
5. Add a rod pocket and bind the quilt.
6. Add any desired bead or button embellishments to the blocks. Stitch a ¼"-diameter button in each corner of the sashing corner posts.
7. Stitch a label to the quilt back.

UNDER THE IVY

LET A BORDER *print be your catalyst for color when choosing the companion fabrics for this quilt. "Meadowlark," a fabric collection by Clothworks (a division of FASCO), featured a graceful scalloped ivy vine filled with birds, nests, and eggs, all in soft spring colors. Even the lattice-print sashing repeated this garden theme.*

Finished Size: 36" x 43"

Materials: *42"-wide fabric*

- 1½ yds. for block background
- ⅛ yd. each or scraps of 12 to 14 assorted fabrics for blocks and pieced border
- ⅜ yd. for sashing
- ⅜ yd. for corner posts and binding
- ¼ yd. for inner border
- 1½ yds. border print for outer border
- 1⅜ yds. for rod pocket and backing
- 42" x 50" piece of batting

Cutting

After cutting the following pieces, use the remaining fabrics in the blocks.

1. From the 12 to 14 assorted block fabrics, cut a minimum of 48 squares, each 1½" x 1½", for the pieced border.
2. From the sashing fabric, cut 5 strips, each 1½" x 42"; crosscut the strips into 42 strips, each 1½" x 4½".
3. From the corner post and binding fabric, cut:
   - 4 strips, each 2" x 42", for binding
   - 1 strip, 1½" x 42"; crosscut the strip to make 28 squares, each 1½" x 1½", for corner posts.
4. From the inner border fabric, cut 4 strips, each 1½" x 42".
5. From the outer border fabric, cut 4 strips, each 7" x 48".

Quilt Top Assembly

1. Using the 4" foundation patterns for the Needles and Notions blocks on pages 28–51, trace 1 each of the 12 patterns, plus 2 additional block patterns of your choice. Trace 1 foundation pattern of Sewing Room Sue—Dreaming and Quilting (pages 53–54).
2. Refer to "Step by Step to Successful Paper Foundation Piecing" (pages 11–17) to construct 14 Needles and Notions blocks and 1 Sewing Room Sue—Dreaming and Quilting block, following the Sewing Order and Fabric Key for each individual block (pages 28–52). Trim "Sue" to 9½" x 14½".

Note: *Sue's original block size was deliberately designed to be larger than necessary so she could be trimmed to fit into a variety of settings.*

3. Arrange the Needles and Notions blocks as desired around the "Sue" block.
4. To make the sashing rows, alternately sew together 5 corner posts and 4 sashing strips, beginning and ending with a corner post. Make 4. In the same manner, stitch a corner post to each end of 4 sashing strips. Press the seam allowances toward the sashing strips.

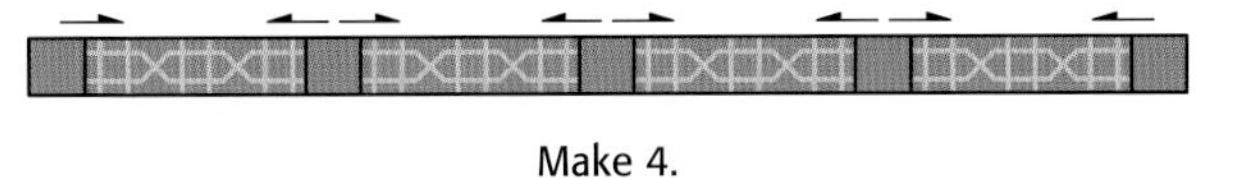

Make 4.

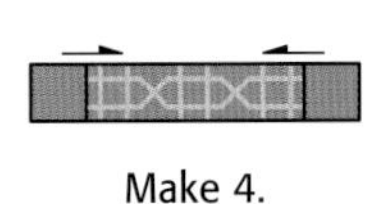

Make 4.

5. To make the block rows, alternately stitch together 4 blocks and 5 sashing strips for the top and bottom rows, beginning and ending with a sashing strip. Stitch a sashing strip to each side of the remaining 6 blocks. Press the seam allowances toward the sashing strips.

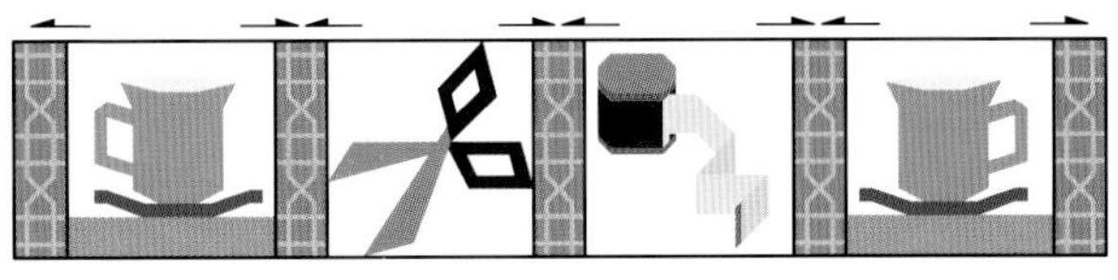

Make 2.

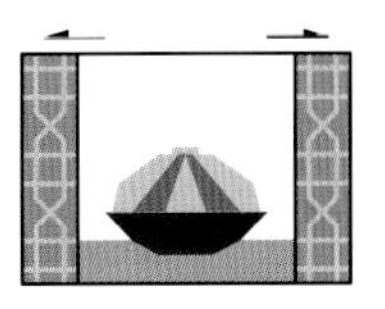

Make 6.

6. Stitch a sashing strip between the 3 blocks on each side of the center block. Stitch the vertical rows to the sides of the "Sue" block. Stitch a sashing row to the top and bottom edges of the top and bottom block rows. Stitch to the top and bottom edges of the center unit.

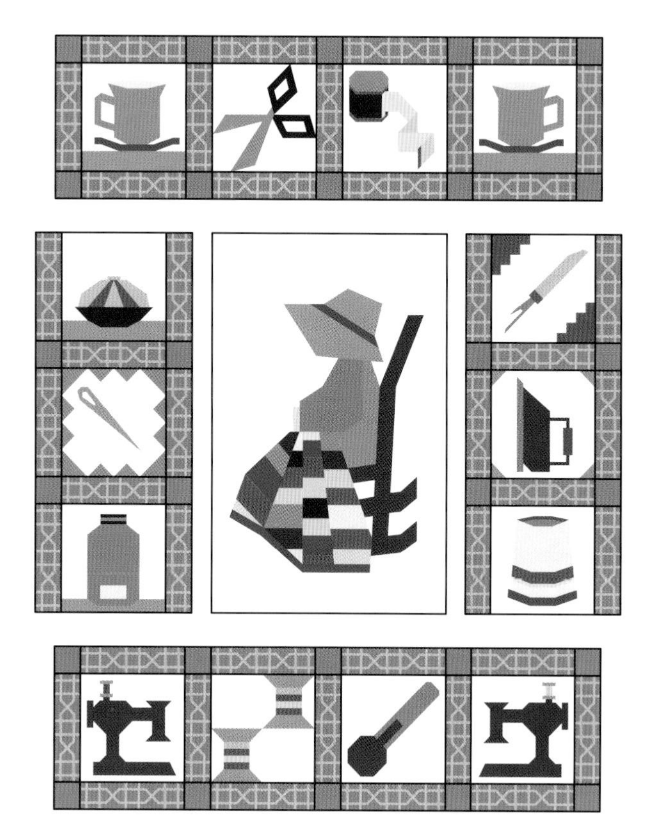

7. Stitch an inner border strip to each side of the quilt; trim the strips even with the top and bottom edges. Stitch the remaining 2 strips to the top and bottom edges; trim the strips even with the sides.

8. Measure the quilt top through the center to determine the width. Using the determined width, stitch together 2 separate rows of pieced border blocks to equal the measurement. You will need approximately 23 to 24 blocks each. Stitch 1 row each to the quilt top and bottom edges.

9. Measure the quilt top for borders as described in "Making Borders with Mitered Corners" on page 20. Cut the border strips to fit, and stitch them to the quilt top, mitering the corners.

Quilt Finishing

Refer to "Finishing Touches" on pages 20–26.

1. Embroider the block details.
2. Layer the quilt top with batting and backing; baste.
3. Quilt as desired.
4. Square up the quilt top.
5. Add a rod pocket and bind the quilt.
6. Add any desired bead or button embellishments.
7. Stitch a label to the quilt back.

SUE—AT THE HEAD OF THE (SEWING) CLASS

ANOTHER BEAUTIFUL BORDER *print sets the stage for this long, narrow wall hanging. Sue, at the head of the "Needles and Notions" class, gathers colors from the surrounding fabrics to stitch into her lap quilt. The sashing strips are actually leftover sections from the border print.*

FINISHED SIZE: 24½" x 60½"

MATERIALS: *42"-wide fabric*

- 1½ yds. for block background
- ⅛ yd. each or scraps of 10 to 12 assorted fabrics for blocks
- ⅜ yd. for sashing
- ⅝ yd. for corner posts and binding
- 2¼ yds. for outer border
- 2 yds. for backing
- 30" x 72" piece of batting

CUTTING

After cutting the following pieces, use the remaining fabrics in the blocks.

1. From the sashing fabric, cut:
   - 4 strips, each 2¼" x 42"; crosscut the strips into 32 sashing strips, each 2¼" x 4½" for the Needles and Notions blocks.
   - 1 strip, 2¼" x 42"; crosscut the strip into 2 side sashing strips, each 2¼" x 12½", and 1 top sashing unit, 2¼" x 10¼", for the "Sue" block

2. From the corner post and binding fabric, cut :
   - 2 strips, each 2¼" x 42"; crosscut the strips into 23 squares, each 2¼" x 2¼", for corner posts
   - 5 strips, each 2" x 42", for binding

3. From the outer border fabric, cut 3 strips, each 6" x 72".

Quilt Top Assembly

1. Using the 4" foundation patterns for the Needles and Notions blocks on pages 28–51, trace 1 each of the 12 patterns. Trace 1 freezer-paper foundation for Sewing Room Sue—Dreaming and Quilting (pages 53–54).

2. Refer to "Step by Step to Successful Paper Foundation Piecing" (pages 11–17) to construct 12 Needles and Notions blocks and 1 Sewing Room Sue—Dreaming and Quilting block, following the Sewing Order and Fabric Key for each individual block (pages 28–52). Using your rotary-cutting equipment, trim "Sue" to 10¼" x 12½".

Note: *Sue's original block size was deliberately designed to be larger than necessary so she could be trimmed to fit into a variety of settings.*

3. Arrange the Needles and Notions blocks in rows of 2 as desired under the "Sue" block.

4. To make the upper sashing row, stitch a corner post to each end of the 2¼" x 10¼" sashing strip. For the remaining sashing rows, alternately sew together 3 corner posts and 2 sashing strips, each 2¼" x 4½", beginning and ending with a corner post. Make 7. Press the seam allowances toward the sashing strips.

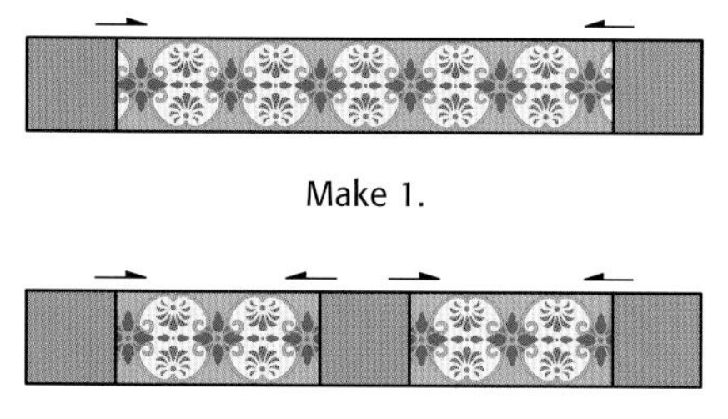

Make 1.

Make 7.

5. To make the block rows, stitch a 2¼" x 12½" sashing strip to the sides of the "Sue" block. For the remaining block rows, alternately stitch together 2 blocks and 3 sashing strips, each 2¼"x 4½", beginning and ending with a sashing strip. Press the seam allowances toward the sashing strips.

6. Stitch the upper sashing row to the upper edge of the "Sue" block. Beginning at the "Sue" block lower edge, alternately stitch the remaining sashing and block rows together, beginning and ending with a sashing row.

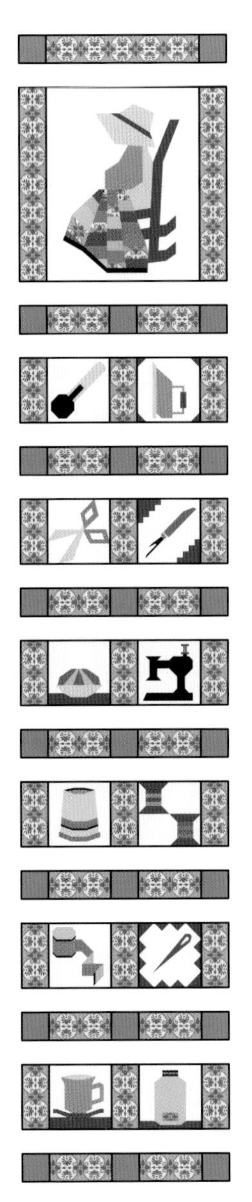

7. Measure the quilt top for borders as described in "Making Borders with Mitered Corners" on page 20. Cut the border strips to fit and stitch them to the quilt top, mitering the corners.

Quilt Finishing

Refer to "Finishing Touches" on pages 20–26.

1. Embroider the block details.
2. Layer the quilt top with batting and backing; baste.
3. Quilt as desired.
4. Square up the quilt top.
5. Add a rod pocket and bind the quilt.
6. Add any desired bead or button embellishments.
7. Stitch a label to the quilt back.

BIBLIOGRAPHY

Bradkin, Cheryl Greider. *Basic Seminole Patchwork.* Mountain View, Calif.: Leone Publications, 1990.

Huff, Jaynette, and Carol Stearle. *Holiday Heroes.* Durango, Colo.: Animas Quilts Publishing, 1996.

Noble, Maurine. *Machine Quilting Made Easy.* Bothell, Wash.: That Patchwork Place, 1994.

ABOUT THE AUTHOR

JAYNETTE HUFF'S interest in quilting began more than twenty-five years ago when she encountered a group of women in an antique store sitting around an old pot-bellied stove. They were laughing and having such fun. When asked what they were doing, they responded, "We're quilting! Want to learn?" The answer was an immediate, "Yes!" Suddenly her life took a turn down another path as quilting began to take up more and more of her attention and focus.

Jaynette's first career was teaching high school English and speech. After completing her master's degree in business administration (MBA) and her course work for her Ph.D. in management, she spent the next twelve years teaching at the college level. It was teaching "Small Business Management" that lead to the next career move: owning and operating her own quilt shop.

Her professional quilting life began in August of 1992 when she opened the quilt shop, Idle-Hour Quilts and Design, in Conway, Arkansas. She has found owning a shop both a joy and a bit overwhelming as she tries to balance running the shop with teaching quilting, designing her own patterns, and quilting her own projects. Her quilts have won several awards and have appeared in numerous quilt magazines and books.

Jaynette Huff lives in Conway with her husband, Larry, their cat, Inky, and Buddy, a miniature schnauzer.